SACRED POETRY
&
MYSTICAL MESSAGES

TO CHANGE YOUR LIFE
&
THE WORLD

PHILLIP ELTON COLLINS

THE ANGEL NEWS NETWORK

SACRED POETRY & MYSTICAL MESSAGES

Copyright © 2012 Phillip Elton Collins

ISBN: 0983143390
ISBN-13: 9780983143390

Contact: info@theangelnewsnetwork.com.

DEDICATION

To Archangels Gabriel, Michael, Raphael, Uriel and Metatron who have always been the foundation of all my teaching and training as a Light Ascension therapist and teacher.

To Ascended Masters El Morya, Lanto, Paul, Serapis Bey, Hilarion, Lady Nada, Lord Sananda and St. Germain. The inspiration you give us to transcend our humanity is what guides my life.

To the Inner Earth Lemurian Council and civilization for opening our eyes to a whole, new world, and some day we becoming one.

To Gaia, Mother Earth. Forgive our abuse. We are awakening. It is not too late, we shall join you in light.

To the Order of Melchizedek for receiving me into your ordination and We Consciousness ministry.

To Jeshua, the Christ Consciousness energies. Your light has always guided my life beyond any belief system.

To Mother Mary and Mary Magdalene. Thank you for assisting in balancing the masculine and feminine energies at this most important time.

To The Angel News Network. With my brothers Jeff Fasano and Joel Anastasi there is no limit to what we can bring out into the world. And to you, Omar Prince, our social media publicist who way shows our word in a most powerful way.

Last, but mostly to my husband James Gozon. A true gift of love and light which I choose to accept with gratitude that allows everything.

"Here on planet Earth you are standing at the brink of the same disasters as past Golden Ages becoming an actual reality. That is why it is so important to start shifting your reality to one that is more compassionate, respectful, and loving of self and each other, and all aspects of creation."

- Thoth, THE EMERALD TABLETS

CONTENTS

ACKNOWLEDGEMENTS

When this latest book began "falling out of me," Actor, playwright and social media publicist, Omar Prince, immediately began organizing the bits and pieces and compiling them into what you see now. Without his efforts there would be no book to go out into the world. He has become an indispensable guardian of my work and that of many others. Omar and Dr. David Spangler, the playwright, and composer, are in the process of adapting my book, *"Coming Home To Lemuria: An Ascension Adventure Story,"* into a stage play as this book goes to press.

In addition to dedicating this book to higher realms, I must also again acknowledge the higher realms that love and support us in our journey. I am so blessed to have them directly involved in my multidimensional life.

Lights on to my fellow cofounders in The Angel News Network, Jeff Fasano and Joel Anastasi, who always create love and support in all the higher realms' truths and teachings we together bring out into the world.

To all my students and teachers in our Modern Day Mystery School who inspire me each day with their courage and commitment to learn new truths about themselves and the world and their willingness to apply them.

To my life partner, James Gozon, who creates an unconditionally loving life and home that makes all things possible.

PREFACE

When something is sacred and mystical it cannot always be explained by known, accepted sources or by our five senses. The words in these poems and messages are filled with ancient wisdom and magic to set us free from ourselves and to awaken us to who we are and why we are here and where we are headed in today's shifting world. After reading the book straight through, open the book to any random page and allow all the mystery of synchronicity to appear for you to receive the words and guidance you were supposed to receive in that moment; that's sacred and mystical. Keep the book visible as a loving reference tool...

The words in this book are not associated with any organized religion or spiritual belief other than the one in your heart. Please use your own resonance and discernment and your path to interpret these words the way you wish. If they resonate, apply them. If not, as my master teacher would say, "Throw them out the preverbal window."

With the intent to be authentic and transparent, may I say I do not take full ownership of the teachings. The words did come from my head and hand, but the concepts are not my ultimate creation. They have actually been passed along for millennia. Many are old ancient wisdoms that may, under my hand, seem new again, knowing nothing is ever new. I have been taught and inspired by many master teachers, and it has all integrated through inspiration here. This book is the product of that process. I no longer know what words come through my mind or other higher sources that have existed for eons. My mind and these sources have finally become one. This book is not about me but 'we' consciousness. Share and use these words as you will... they belong to all of us and are intended to raise us to a higher state of being.

Most important of all, it's not about the source of these words but about you enjoying the journey of the sacred and mystical word, allowing these words to inspire you the way they came to and through me. If that takes place, we shall join in oneness and love. I dedicate these words to all the people and higher beings that have inspired these words during this crucial time of change within our world and ourselves.

To know, to dare, to do, to serve, and to be,
In Love and Light,
Phillip Elton Collins

PART ONE

SACRED POETRY

I.
TWELVE COSMIC CONCEPTS OF CONSCIOUSNESS (THREE CS)

✿

Twelve Star Systems 'seeded' planet Earth
Through these systems we gained great girth.
Each star system gave a gift
Which allows us to manifest a swift shift.
This gift is known as three sees (Three Cs):
Cosmic Concepts of Consciousness,
And they are always amongst us.

(1) To resonate and apply
UNIVERSAL LAW,
That heals me consciousness,
Allowing we consciousness to apply.

Creating unity and oneness,
Eliminating the distress of
Separation, confrontation and duality,
So they are no longer a reality.

(2) To LEARN TO LOVE,
Is the sacred mission of Mother Earth,
First love of self,
Allows all the rest.
To stop judging, shaming and blaming,
And apply unconditional love,
For the God in me is the same as thee.

To know what we resist; persists.

Through this Love-er-versity
You will end adversity,
And create the next Golden Age,
All before was just a stage.

(3) To ACCEPT WITH COMPASSION,
Thus forgive self,
And see all others, as brothers.

To balance giving and receiving,
As an essential part
In our discovery and recovery.

(4) To SEE THE MEANING, VALUE AND
PURPOSE,
OF ALL LIFE.
To see all strife as a chosen way
To know your way.
To awaken your soul plan,
That allows us to stand.

(5) To FILL OUR HEARTS WITH GRATITUDE
For all the fortitude and multitude
Everywhere, for everyone,
That has brought and sought
In our choosing with no losing.

(6) To commit to a PERSONAL PROCESS
Of an in-depth examine of self
To know how self relations
Effects all relations and nations.

To be responsible for our responses,
And reactions,
To know the difference,
Without defiance.

(7) To know our BODY TEMPLE
Is not simple,
Housing our emotional, mental and physical bodies.
To have gratitude for the platitudes
Of these three aspects,
That are awakening the
Concept of Consciousness.

(8) To SURRENDER TO THE UNKNOWN,
Knowing all probabilities and possibilities,
Lie within,
To know the value of the void,
In order to avoid not knowing.

(9) To BE IMPECCABLE,
Authentic and transparent with WORD,
Preparing for telepathy
Where there aptly will be
No deceit, nor denial of the deceit,
Won't that be neat?
Supporting our soul plan.

(10) To know the Universe
WOULD BE INCOMPLETE
Without each of you, a version.
Knowing being complete,
In self,
Is the source of the universe.

(11) To know WE TEACH WHAT WE NEED TO
LEARN,
This way we earn
Our way back to higher realms.
No one knows more than another,
Through your talents and gifts
We all further consciousness.

(12) To know the essential deed
Of creating COMMUNITIES OF
EQUALITY, HARMONY AND BALANCE,
Of giving and receiving,
These are the deeds of life.

2.

OATH OF THE LIGHT
WORKER AND WAY SHOWER

ADAPTED FROM THE ANGEL NEWS NETWORK

We are all light workers
To a greater or lesser extent,
It merely depends on your bent.

You have a mission and purpose
In this lifetime.
And if you so choose,
It is time to release the conceal and reveal
The various healing modalities
That are your true realities.

You may partake in those modalities,
Any way you choose,
There is no way to lose.

Some may work with individuals or groups
In certain techniques,

And that remains your mission and purpose,
Feeling quite complete.

Way showers are light workers
Who bring their gifts and talents
Out into the world in a larger way,
That is their pay.

A way shower shows the way
For others to move onto their path,
With no wrath,
To create communities,
Of equality, harmony and balance,
So there is no malice.

You may ask, at last:
Am I a lighter worker?
Am I a way shower?
How can I know?
Am I both, not to boast.

Some will know this total purpose now,
Others need time for it to reveal,
And that's no crime to let it be real.
Not to worry,
It will all be defined and refined
As you continue your journey,
For life is a continuous refinery.

You are all on the path of the light worker,
Some may choose to remain where you are,
Others will go further far,
To support self,
And that of another.

If and when you are steady,
And ready to take the oath of both
The light worker and way shower,
The heavens will shower their Light on you,
No matter what you decide to do.

3.
THE FIVE
AGREEMENTS

ADAPTED FROM THE ANGEL NEWS NETWORK

From the Archangelic mission of Michael,
Through trance channel Jeff Fasano
Comes something called,
THE FIVE AGREEMENTS,
Blasting into the Earth plane's vibrato.

For those who so chose,
These Agreements are leads
To WORLD SERVICE, indeed.

While they number from one to five,
We shall start at the bottom,
To arrive at the top,
In order to know,
It's a bottom to top teaching
That allows us reaching the top,
Where we stop at World Service.

RECEIVING LOVE is Agreement number five,
It's all about being alive,
Allowing self to power our ability
To be who we are,
In order to receive love of self,
To take our love off the shelf,
In order to love others.

When we love self,
We no longer need to look
Outside our self, to love,
Nor hold others responsible
For the love we now choose
To give our self.

We're now not giving to get,
But balance giving and receiving,
Yet.

When we come from living,
Giving and receiving love,
Our talents and gifts
Come from a place
Of total grace.
We can then be
The person we chose to be,
And create the life we want,
Without any strife or knife.

Agreement number four is

About learning more to
DEVELOP A SENSE OF SELF,
Which is often lost in the strife of life.

This is an agreement
To move into the depth,
Of our heart, to begin the start
To know, love and value,
Self enough,
So we may develop the strength,
And courage to contribute
Our talents and gifts to the world,
In tribute to who we are,
And create the life,
We choose to live,
Forever more.

Agreement three is to focus on
WHAT IS IN YOUR LIFE?
Rather than what we perceive is not.
This can help us all a lot.
For many of us we would rather complain
About what is not, allowing things to stay the same.

Focusing on 'what is' creates gratitude,
Which manifests abundance,
And helps create new opportunities,
Creating multitudes.

Through our unique talents and gifts,
Along with qualities of self,
We critique creation.

Focusing on what is not
Is a trap with no way back,
Forcing us to look outside ourselves,
For what we think we lack.

The raw material we say we need to
Create the life we say we want
Has and always will be, within us,
A plenty.

Agreement two, (COMMIT TO A PERSONAL
PROCESS), is all about you,
And your willingness to examine,
The me in the we.

For the leading cultural curse in humanity now,
Is that most of our leaders and followers
Are bringing the unhealed me,
Into the we.

What a different world it would be
If the me were eliminated from the we.

Moving our consciousness
From me to we
Requires, of course, moving the me,
Out of the we.

The narcissistic me
Constantly seeks to be validated,
Gratified and celebrated,
At the expense of the we.

The me consciousness traps us,
And wraps us in lack and limitation.
The we consciousness, in contrast,
Provides a path of full lives,
Without any condemnation.

Living life fully requires.
Knowing who you are,
And having a strong sense of self,
So you may serve the world,
Through the whirl of your
Unique talents and gifts.

As we move into we consciousness
We really know and show
We can balance giving and receiving
All along the road in relationships,
That services the highest good of all,
With no failure.
In order to create and maintain and sustain

We consciousness it requires
A perpetual PERSONAL PROCESS,
Dealing with issues,
To help you release old behavior patterns,
That no longer matter,
And keep you locked in lack and limitation,
Of the limiting me.

When we agreed to take
Responsibility for the me
Through a continuous process of the me,
Then we can see, honor and value,
And love our self enough,
To love our divine soul plan,
And serve the world,
With no fanfare.

Now you can see all
Previous agreements have
Lead to thee,
To choose or not,
Agreement number one.
TO COMMIT TO WORLD SERVICE,
In the we.

To use your talents and gifts,
To eliminate all myths,
To raise the level of resonance,

And vibration of ourselves,
And communities,
In order to create,
A new world,
Of equality and harmony,
That the world has never seen...

4.
THE SIX
SACRED MESSAGES

ADAPTED FROM THE ANGEL NEWS NETWORK

We have Four Agreements there.
And Five Agreements here,
And now Six Sacred Messages near,
That's fifteen words of wisdom
Coming through.
Wow, something, someone,
Really wishes to bring teachings,
A new.

It all has to do with
Something called Ascension
Where our planet has chosen
Something new.

To raise her vibration so
She may become a star,
Requiring everything within and upon

Her body to not go far,
But to also choose to bask
In her divine light,
With all our might.

From Jeshua to Jeffrey,
The "Js" are the same,
A fifth dimensional divine message
From and through the two,
To share the Christ Consciousness energy,
So we can reduce our shame and blame.

Jeffrey is the trance channel messenger
That this came through,
And Jeshua is the frequency
Whose intention it is to make things,
A new.

The teacher and the lessons
Are here to support our
Connecting with our divinity,
Allowing the compassionate healing
Of our wounds and defenses,
So we have no need of being defensive,
Ever again.
These six ascended messages
Are given to us,
So we may look into reflection,
And within ourselves,
See a connection of where we are now.

These teachings are to support
Our ascension process,
Moving to a higher plane,
From a transition within,
That prevents us from being the same.

Many billions of us are here
To bring these teachings near,
To create a new world paradigm,
Of no not.

These six submissions
Compound and build upon themselves,
So we may create
A new self, and new world bordering,
On love.

These sacred sparkles
Glitter day and night
Releasing major issues,
For you to gain further insight.

We shall briefly mention each lesson
With a simple explanation,
And for further review,
We ask you to go to
The Angel News Network
For an in-depth study and renew.

(1) WHO ARE YOU?
Fully knowing who you are,
And why you are here,
Are quite essential in the ascension invention.

(2) THE POWER OF ALONENESS
It's all about being able to be alone
Without being lonely.
Through the loving relationship with self,
You can stand in your divine inner
Power in any hour of the day.
Examine the relationships you are having
In regard to your life's mission,
Moving to a place of power, now.

This lesson is about bringing,
You to yourself.

(3) RELEASING, DUALITY, ISOLATION AND SEPARATION
Oh, how we love to hold on to these.
Let us now surrender them to a gentle breeze.

How much time is consumed
Opposing what is outside of us,
Rusting in fear.

Are we even using
Our spirituality to further
Separate and isolate.

Thus creating duality.

It is time to release these negatives
To allow positive to flourish,
In the me, moving the we,
Consciousness.

(4) THE POWERFULNESS OF YOU
The time has come to move into
The depth of your heart,
And start to fully,
See and be.
The powerfulness of me,
Can be in this place,
There is no race.

This is a serene power,
A deep knowingness of being
That is ready to see
You no longer have to prove
Who you are,
To be loved,
Just be.

(5) WHERE ARE YOU NOW?
From time to time you become
Sidetracked from your purpose.
These messages bring you back,
And take out the lack,
So you are on course

To where you know you
Need to be.

Are you now being who you are,
Releasing and policing what no longer resonates.
Are you moving through a
Personal process,
To arrest the old you,
And support your highest goal.

(6) ARE YOU READY?
Are you ready to leave the old behind?
And apply what's surfaced
In the first five messages,
To bury the old,
And birth a new you,
Even if that means stepping
Into the unknown, alone.

Are you ready to be who you are?
Are you ready to be a star?
Are you ready to take whatever
Step it takes to be you.

5.
THE 'I AM' PRESENCE

What is this thing, this force called the I AM?
What exactly is present in this name?
A force, a presence that has no shame nor blame.

We hear The Christ, and the name Saint Germain,
Associated with this, the same.

Does anyone truly understand this name,
That has neither shame nor blame?
Let us now attempt to explain...

The I AM seems ancient in its claim
To have created all in this domain.
By the mere spoken word the power of creation
Is released in elaboration.

But since we are part of creation,
This I AM force is part of our self-relation.

The promise of this power
We are told is our, forever more.

Whatever follows the words I AM,
Life forces give mirth to the birth.

I AM first vibrates in the brain,
Followed by the flesh it becomes, the same.

I AM THAT I AM is also my name,
And I can know I am connected to all, with no shame.

It is the imperishable, eternal,
Individual identity of every human being,
Rather than doing, just being.

Perhaps, I AM is just what humanity needs,
To know it is already divine perfection, indeed!

6.
A RAGE WITHIN

What mysterious opiate origin lies deep within humanity's ancestral rage?

From whence its ancient source that can kill and conquer, we ask?

It lives deep within us all. And yet it can frighten us when it reveals its cruel countenance in duality and confrontation.

What is the cause, knowing its effect, of this monstrous force, we ask?

The moment is upon us to understand, release, and heal this ugly anger from our being that has kept us imprisoned so long...

Dear Souls, this ragged rage comes from our so many Golden Ages, loss. Loss due our 'mighty minds' that thought they could control creation, replace it, be it.

A fierce force came upon us that could not, would
not accept and trust our divinity, and connection to
creation; whence once we could.

As humanity went its own way, deep within we knew
we had lost something most precious. We became
enraged at self for being so selfish, so foolish.

This self-rage has reflected out, and created the much
madness in our world for millennium.

Throughout the eons we have carried this
self-sabotaging sense, and inflicted it upon self, each other,
and our unconditionally loving home, Mother Earth.

Dear Souls, the time has come to accept with
compassion, thus forgive how we have chosen to learn
through our freedom of will and choice.

It is time to re-connect with Creation. To know we are
a divine aspect of it.

We have travelled as far from the truth as possible. Let
us now turn around and head home...

When now, at last again we consciously connect with
creation, our rage shall ramble away like an angry child
replaced by cosmic love, as adults.

For only through our connection to creation can we embrace our final Golden Age in service to ALL THERE IS.

Are we ready to release our furious face, and create a world knowing we are god experiencing self? An equal, balanced world without the angry 'me', replaced by the loving 'we'...

7.
OUR GREATNESS

Humankind walks in the forgetting of our Greatness,
Not remembering what Power and Knowledge lies
within each of our souls.

We walk through Life unaware of our Talents and Gifts,
Seeking secrets already known within us.

We are Eternal Beings of Light,
Awaiting our Awakening and En-light-en-ment.

Wisdoms once known will now awaken
Within each of us in World Service,
If we so choose in our observance.

All that ever was and still is
Is waiting to be born in WE CONSCIOUSNESS,
If we can just get the me out of the we,
Creating worlds of equality, and harmony.

Are you ready?
I AM.

8.
AMERICA,
THE NEW GOLDEN AGE

From ancient scrolls from afar
Comes new knowledge to many
That this 'land of plenty'
Will now prompt
A New Golden Age, so many
Will truly have much plenty.

America was once a Land of Great Light
And might, eons ago.
And nothing now
Can prevent Her spiritual activation
To rise, again, and create Her true nation.

So now beloved America,
In the not-so-distant future
Through your Real Inner Being
And the will of your people and seeing
You will create a brilliant spiritual steeple, like no
other...

For you are a Land of Light
That your forefathers not forgot your past brightness.
Now, no matter how it may appear
You are very near and will again blaze
Brilliant as the sun
Being a new son for all nations.

America you are strong within,
Your mind and body,
Stronger than you think.
You are destined
To rise up
And be a new world link, to creation,
As an unconditionally loving nation...to all nations of
this world.

For America you have a destiny
Of great import.
And we who have watched
Over you for centuries, The Beings of Light,
Delight at your awakening,
And shift back into our Light.

One by one great awakened souls
Are coming who know their God-Power
In this hour of your summing.
Thus another Golden Age cometh
Upon the Earth
And it will be maintained and sustained
By your America love, for eons more...

9.
WHAT WE CALL DEATH

Death is feared.
And yet ever so near.
Let us re-train ourselves
Through another view
And review a new view
Of what we call death.

Death is but an opportunity
For rest and re-attunement,
To free us from the out-of-tunement,
Turmoil and imbalances of being Earth-bound,
Long enough to heal enough
To decide if we want another ride
On the physical side.

Perhaps physical format's only reason to be
Is for preparing, perfecting our human body
For another toddy, mixing and blending with its
Spiritual body, once again.

Maybe this reunion with spirit
Is the real reason for human experience,
At all.

When a loved one has passed on
They are actually with their higher body
consciousness,
Causing celestial bliss.

If we could only remember
Our body is only a wardrobe,
We wear for a moment,
Until we shed it,
To accept a better opportunity to bed,
A fuller moment.

It is the unknowing of these truths
Which hamper humanity and keep
Us in self-created chains of non-clarity.

We get stuck and refuse
To understand the true cycle of life,
Dragging ourselves into stiff with self-pity,
Breaking down our resistance,
Creating more persistence in the resistance,
And what we resist, persists.

It is the lack of knowing our
True spiritual composition
That keeps us in the position

Of lack and limitation.
Let us celebrate and emulate
The fact that we are eternal beings.
Who can never die,
And when we leave these bodies,
Which we have done thousands of times before,
We shall mourn never more,
Knowing we have gloriously returned home,
To decide what our next roam, ride and home,
Shall be.

10.
HOW TO BE
AN ASCENDED MASTER, FASTER

The creative life forces within our bodies
Are to be raised into
The crown of your head,
And instead of flowing down,
Are to flow up in recognition, instead,
Of your I AM Presence,
Which is always around.

Then through awakened oneness,
Thoughts and emotions,
Needing nothing else,
We can conceive creative works
At the mental and emotional levels
Through the creation of equality,
Harmony and balance,
With the alliance of
Idealistic ideas, ideals of art,

Imagination and invention,
That serves and blesses,
All our intention.

With this constructive consciousness
The physical body can remain,
Eternally youthful and beautiful
Being the image and likeness,
And brightness of the God-likeness, within.

Once we achieve immorality,
And creator consciousness,
Our true mission begins,
As the ascended master, faster,
Mending the past, we awaken at last,
And feel the good God-force, again.

Feeling gloriously connected
To perfection and true direction
Our true divine soul plan, begins...

II.
AREN'T WE TIRED OF GROWING OLD YET?

We know the cells in our body
Are not so oddly programmed for eternal life.
So why don't we honor our cell design,
And live all the time.

Higher realms are quite puzzled
Why humanity continues its struggle
Of self-created lack and limitation
Where we insist upon decay and disintegration.

It is quite puzzling how humanity
Is blind as to why our bodies and mind
Seem to continue to fold and grow old.

So if our cells can eternally renew
Why can't you?
Why do we as a race,
Seem content to continue death,
At such a good pace?

While we clasp to youth,
And beauty and life,
We still hold onto our strife.
So what we cling to most,
Can't be boasted in life.

Just maybe it all has to do
With our losing our connection
To our Inner-Power-Presence,
While looking outside self,
For all the inside message.

And let us also balance and check
Our immobilizing emotions and terrorizing thoughts,
At the door, that's a good idea too,
Then we'll never have to grow old, anymore.

12.

ABOUT AMERICA

All nations are divine expressions
Of creation's diversified revelations.

But America for most of her people,
Is much more than they ever dreamed, it seems.

America is an expression of
Divine inclusiveness of mankind
To aspire to reflect ALL THERE IS,
In like kind.

Remember the Founding Fathers' inspirations
Through their founding papers,
Those were never fully fathomed.

America is the heart chakra,
And center,
Of the spiritual aspirations,
Of Mother Earth, not excluding all her nations.

Through America's creation,
As a nation,
The firm foundation of the
Cosmic Christ Consciousness,
The three sees (3Cs),
Will land in mankind's hearts,
And become be's.

No matter how things seem now,
In our social and political nature,
This Mighty Light is in the process
Of growing and expanding throughout Earth's purpose.

Fasten your seat belts,
Many wondrous things,
Will be taking place,
As the old paradigm melts.

Miracles are not a thing of the ancient past,
But very present in the now, at last.

We are entering
The Age of Miracles, again,
Revealing the glories
Of the magic stories of the old,
New again.

For America is the consciousness
For this planet.
Reflecting the planetary soul plan, in effect,
Planted in the cosmic concept of consciousness,
That is here, at long last.

13.
THE PSYCHIC/ASTRAL WORLD

People are entertained, and enthralled by various
Aspects of the psychic world.
It gives people a thrill
To think something other than this life,
Exists, at will.

Our now emotional, mental and physical bodies
Live in what is called the third dimension (3D).
When we sleep or first die, we go to the fourth
dimension (4D):
The psychic or astral world.
That's how it's configured, y'all.

Beyond the psychic (4D) is 5D, the fifth dimension,
Many marvelous spiritual truths and wisdoms
Are housed from these much higher realms,
And continue to enlighten and delight us.

The psychic frequency contains
The reflection and connection of humanity generated

By imbalanced emotions and thoughts,
And oughts of our individual personal lives.
You have many TV shows created and brought
Around these attachments to the human drama.

Within the psychic realm
The daily activities of feelings,
Thoughts and body reign supreme,
And continue to tangle and dangle us,
Often preventing the creative
Growth and expansion of life.

Many ascended masters through
Their acceptance and compassion for
The lethargic evolution of humanity,
Through the psychic realm,
Want to clear and cleanse the psychic plane,
And give humanity a new start.

There is no teaching nor reaching for higher truths
Within the psychic realm,
There is merely fascination
That only shares a small part
Of the grand life plan.

Let us continue to focus our true higher being,
On Higher Beings,
Reflecting and supporting our higher selves,

Clearing and cleansing our self,
Being our higher self,
Being the bright light,
With all our might.

14.
WHY WE DIE

Within our inner being
A life stream flows
Through our physical body.
This stream is a gift from above.
Like water in a stream,
This life stream runs through our pineal,
As no menial task filling our nerves.

The nerves beat our heart,
And that gets everything started.
This permits walking and talking,
And chalking it all up to
The energizing light, often called,
The silver cord,
The accounts and accords the life, we know.

At so-called death,
This silver cord cuts,
And the stream of life,

Stops in its tracks,
And the body stops, as well.

But the real reason things finally stop,
Is due to the waste of life energy,
Through-uncontrolled feelings and thoughts
That cause, not so oddly, the disintegration of all our
bodies.

The life stream simply slips away,
From the top of the head,
With the silver cord cut,
We are really dead,
As the heart finally ceases to beat,
And we are complete in that lifetime.

15.

TAKING OUR POWER BACK

❦

Once upon a time through
The abuse of our power
We lost our power
In order to regain it in a new hour,
Now.

We were connected to
ALL THERE IS,
But that wasn't enough.
Through freedom of will and choice
We thought our minds
Could make a better choice.

For eons in our 'mind field,'
We've learned a lot about,
What is,
Through what is not.

Now the mind is returning
To the heart,

And we are ready,
To start a new start.

Let us re-connect,
And correct and connect,
To ALL THERE IS, in effect.

Only through a renewed true connect
Can we correct our forgetfulness,
And create heartfelt consciousness.

Once awake,
We shall remember,
Who we are,
Why we are here,
And take our power back,
And never throw it back,
As true divine beings,
Being ALL THERE IS.

16.
AUTHENTICITY
AND INTEGRITY

Where did authenticity,
And integrity,
Go?

Did they run away because
They have no place to go or be?
Was it because the we got lost.
In the me?

In advanced civilizations
Everyone is telepathic,
So transparency prevents deceit,
And all meet in authentic celebrity.

The governments, religions and corporations
That think they control the world
Are lacking truth, and stacking untruths,
A plenty.

People often say one thing,
And do another,
Confounding and confusing even one another.

There is much deceit,
And denial of that deceit,
Keeping us incomplete.

Truth is,
Governance is more effective
When we truly care,
And wish to share the truth.

None of us has all the answers,
Let's simply ask what others need,
And execute deeds
Of the highest good of all.

Let us leave the old paradigm
Of fear, greed, and control,
And mold a new reality
Based on authenticity and integrity,
And finally leave the old.

17.
AN INTERNAL GYRO SYSTEM: RESONANCE

We have a gifted gyro system
In each of us.
It is a must that we use it,
Or we lose it,
And experience the consequence.

The system is called resonance.
It's how you feel about something,
To determine dissonance or not.

It is a vibrational frequency
Of a person, place or thing,
That will determine
If you have a similar ring,
Or frequency.

The ability to use resonance
Is a key component
In the moment of expanding
Your discernment, awareness and fairness.

18.
CREATION OF PLANET EARTH

The entire cosmic universe
Was involved and ignited
In the creation of planet Earth.

Twelve Star systems came together
To bring the best of each star
Into our reach from afar.

It was called the grand divine experiment
Inspired by unconditional love,
So they called us,
The Lover-versity of Love.

The whole universe is waiting
And watching us now
To see if we can ace this
Final place, the final Golden Age.

To learn to love self and another is the mission
In order to become the master teachers

And preachers of love,
And be the love stuff of submission.

In recent years we have discovered
Billions of galaxies,
Many like us.
Needing to learn like us
About the reality of love.

Are we ready to accept
That this immense galactic universe
Is not adverse to a total
Connection through affection.

19.
BELIEF AND KNOWING

The mind believes,
The heart knows,
So sayeth, our soul.

Beliefs change,
But truth remains the same,
Is the game.

Those who intend to know,
Will know.
Those who believe often
Get locked into a mindset
That is difficult to unset
And can cripple their ability
To see beyond the net of the mind,
Often eluding truth's upset.

You are the one deciding your destiny,
Through freedom of choice and will.
So keep your mind and heart open.

Ask questions, explore the unknown,
Until it becomes the known.

Now the mind is moving
Back into service to the heart,
Being vice versa for a long time,
Knowing where that got us.

Now we shall experience truth,
Without being thrown
Under the bus!

20.

OUR TRUE STATE OF BEING

In reality formless best describes
Our true state of beingness.

Right now I am housing my formlessness,
In a human body,
But oddly enough
I am almost ready to set that form
Aside and ride away
And decide another day,
If I'll come this way, again.

One's form serves only a brief respite
While relates to the journey
One supports,
In a particular point in time,
And port.

No matter what form I choose,
I can never really lose

Knowing I AM,
One with ALL THERE IS,
Which includes the entire
Molecular cosmic experience.

21.

THE SPHINX

Profound mystery still surrounds
The great Sphinx of Egypt.

It is time to know the truth
About this lion head,
And human body,
That oddly enough continues
To confound everybody.

The Sphinx was built during the time
Of the Great Pyramid of Egypt.
It was constructed by architects
From an Inner Earth frequency,
Using sound frequencies
That we know not of now.

In order for the Communication Center
Of the Pyramid to be complete
It needed the electromagnetic connection
From the heart of the Sphinx.

Although that connection is broken
The Sphinx still is a powerful
Central point on Earth, to be a token,
That aligns us with our galactic center.

The time to reboot the Sphinx
Is near.
So let us not fear,
Being ready to live in peace
Which is the purpose of
The Sakabama Goddess,
Whom the Sphinx was built for.
Now she can continue to be the guardian
Of all earth pyramids,
Forever more.

22.
TELLING THE TRUTH

Think of the money and time
We could save
If everyone was telling the truth.

And never mind not being able to trust,
With such little truth in the roost.

The world is filled with deceit,
And the denial of that deceit.
It's become a not so neat cultural norm,
To twist another's arm.

Through the evolution of consciousness
We are breaking down old controls,
And old paradigm roles,
Those no longer apply.

Even ancient scrolls are new again
Revealing what needs to be healed again,
In the now.

The ancient truths teach and tell
That being true, or not,
Reveals the real you.

Archangelic, Inner Earth and Star Realms, too,
Are now assisting in creating the new,
Telling the truth,
All the time.

23.
EYES OF MY HEART

Beloved Weary, Wonderful World,
It is Time to take the Is from Thee,
And replace I, and Me,
So then we can really see,
The We.

The Way we shall be in in order to see,
Is through Opening The Eyes of Thy Heart!

For eons our Mind has ruled the World,
And now through opened Heart Eyes,
My Mind can serve my Heart,
So that we shall never part, again.

The Time has come to quiet the Mental Body,
So through the Neutral Heart
There will be no need for fought.

The Love of Self is the true Quest,
And we shall never rest,
Until true intimacy is abreast, dear ones.

Now through The Lessons of Life,
We shall stop judging and blaming and creating strife,
So with new, opened eyes, and Lovingness,
We shall finally know Oneness.

24.
THE MYTH OF DUALITY

Duality is a myth!
A taught, learned condition
Which has kept us miffed, for eons.

When we raise our consciousness to oneness
This illusion of life
Becomes noneness.

Moving from the me to the we awareness
Spares us the continued pain
Which we no longer need to maintain and sustain.

Have not we learned all we need to learn
From separation, isolation and confrontation?

The truth is, the myth of duality
No longer needs to exist,
Nor persist.

25.

IN GRATITUDE
TO ST. GERMAIN, FOR AMERICA

St. Germain, most folks in America
Know you not,
That you are the great loving force behind
Our nation's soul plan-terria.

For centuries this truth was known in the East,
And now it comes forth to the West,
So we shall now know you best.

Your great masterful presence in Europe,
Alleviating much suffering,
Gave way to America's buffering.

America's very freedom, in the beginning
Was the result of your tireless efforts,
Protecting and encouraging those responsible
For our very beginning, and sending.

The drafting of the Declaration of Independence
Was a direct result of your love,
You being our freedom's dove.

Now more surely we know of your
Untiring efforts and work,
That saved us from other's yoke.

As we draw ever closer, and closer,
Our love through our knowing,
We accept with gratitude
Your being the 'Bearer of Light,'
Of our glowing.

26.
THE GRACE OF GOD'S GOLD

You think you know what gold is,
It is something to wear,
Something of show biz.

You think gold is a means of exchange,
Or for ornamentation.
Well, let us tell you something of gold
You might think strange.

Gold is placed upon our planet for many uses,
And many abuses.

Gold grows within the Earth,
Like a plant,
Vitalizing and balancing into the ground,
Allowing us to be sound.

Gold's greatest activity and purpose,
Is to release its energy,
Thus, balance the atomic synergy, on the surface.

It feeds all of nature,
And all that we need.

Gold is the sun's energy
Feeding the interior and exterior
Activities of the inferior.

Gold is placed within the Earth
By the Lords of Creation,
Great Beings of Love and Light.

Gold's energy is really radiant
Electronic force from the sun,
In a dense ray,
To keep denser energy away.

Some sunny day,
Not far away,
You will be able to manifest
Gold's ray through your thoughts
In a normal way.

Then you will know
The only true use of gold
Is to support the good of the whole,
Beyond the consciousness of old.

27.
TO LOVE
SELF THROUGH BEAUTY

We've all experienced Beauty
In a sunset, face or space.
But have you ever wondered
Why does beauty take place?

Perhaps, the answer lies in how it makes you feel.
What sensations race through your Being
When you are seeing
Something truly real?

Beloveds, Beauty is the True,
Expression
Of the Mighty God-force inside you!

The energy of this mighty force
Allows you to see,
The perfection in Thee.

The Heart races, your nerves tingles in places,
When you see beauty,
In a single person, place or thing.

In effect, Dear Ones,
You are falling in love with you.
You then realize you are that Love,
Through your new light view.

You can then choose
To take that loving-you-beauty
And use it as a mirror, a reflection
Of an essential inner aspect
Of your new divine self-respect.

To love one's self through beauty,
Is the greatest God-force duty
You can ever Be.

For loving self through beauty,
Now frees us in our new duty
To Love All,
Once and for All.

28.
TRUE MAGIC AS
AN ASCENDED MASTER

Do you want to know true magic?
Then let me explain,
The Ascended Master's domain...

An Ascended Master is a magical manner
Whose Self-empowerment, through consciousness
Breaks the human veil
And brings true life and wisdom, well.

Through their choices and training
They are trusted with great cosmic forces
Beyond humanity's framing, and taming.

Thus, all forces and things
Obey their command.
Because they are Self-Conscious Beings,
Not just being man.
The Ascended Master can control

All the manipulation of Light
Through their bright might.

It is through the outpouring of Light,
That an Ascended Master is able
To share for those in the stable
Of their care.

They are constantly
Pouring out rays of Light
To vanish and dissolve
Our limitation and lack of the Light,
Like a fog in the night.

The Ascended Master gives
Protection to persons, places, things and conditions
Many times over.

While we are totally oblivious
To their givingness.

Thus, there can be no gratitude
For the attitude of their giving.
While the Master gives,
Not to get.
They can change their bodies
Through cellular re-structuring,
And conscious atomic control
Like we in a player's role.

The Ascended Master has freed them selves
From our thoughts and feelings,
That have kept us reeling, for eons.

They are all powerful manifestors,
Of all substance and energy,
Including the four elements
Are at their willing and bidding.

These Glorious Beings who guard
And help us
Are all-knowing and all-seeing,
Because they bring forth
The God-Self Within, Being
Through their Super Humanness
Perfection, Love, and Light, as their bright right.

Let us now awaken
The Great Inner God-Self
Within each of us, like the Ascended Masters,
So we shall be free, ever after.

29.
WAY OF THE WARI

There once was the Way of the Wari,
Who have now left us in a bit of a worry.
Who exactly were these ancient folks?
What were their original yolks?
And how now can we truly
Know these amazing blokes?

There are artful artifacts for sure of Wari,
But they only tell part of the story.
Let us 'connect' with them now,
For they continue to exist
In what we would call eternal mist.

Conventional wisdom says Wari was pre-Inca
But perhaps this is just part of our inkling
To know more of this indigenous I AM.

Let us review and contrast
What we know and don't know,

About this glorious past,
And fill in some blanks, at long last.

Scholars may baulk at some of our sources,
But let us create and combine courses,
So we can stay open,
To integrate sources, and create new forces.

The story we know as Wari
Began with what we think was pre-Inca,
But can you be open and let us explain
More of their history's additional domain.

So for some we must meander in myth
For others this will be true grit
In order for all the pieces to fit.

Long before your recorded history
In the land of mist and mystery
Lies our great true history.

It was a time when we were directly connected
To ALL THERE IS.
And great powers beyond
Assisted our existence.
The few wonder-filled artifacts left
Reveal only part of the mystery
Veiled in their hidden history.

The time has come for you
To know more of our true tracks...

Their powers and skills came
Far beyond our physical domain.

Their spiritual and cultural leaders
Were taught from previous advanced civilizations
In order for them to create new revelations.

From Lemuria, Atlantis and Egypt, too
Great teachings and telepathic language were brought
through.

The time has come for us to see
The true connection
In all of we.

This Story of Wari will further be told
In The Museum of Art's Show
Revealing much more than the old.

30.
LOVE AND LIGHT

The Light is God's way
Of creating and maintaining and sustaining
Peace and Perfection through Creation.
It is the way of showing us
The clear Light of day.

The transcendent and magnificent
Actives of Love and Light
Are the ways to show us
Our manifested might.

Man never ceases creating
Through love and light, his God-Self.
Transcending the little self- elf,
Of lacking and limiting.

Let us choose to live
At the Center of our Being
In light and love,
Surpassing any surgery of the soul.

Light forgives all mistakes
Of the human self.
Acceptance and compassion
Is all that it takes.

31.
BROTHERHOOD
OF MOUNT SHASTA

Echoed within the mysteries of Mount Shasta,
It is said there is a Brotherhood,
That is a kin to the Great White Fatherhood,
An unbroken lineage
From very ancient privilege.

There are many rumors, myths and legends
That remains unanswered of their origin.
So let us at least ponder the meaning and purpose
Of this Brotherhood of Shasta,
And ask what exactly are they after.

It is to remind and teach us, again
We are created
In the image and likeness of God.
That we are being God,
Being us, and there is not sin.
The mass of mankind continues
To struggle within their hearts

That they are the giver and receiver
Of all parts.

The Eternal Law of Life,
Teaches,
What you think and feel creates,
All strife,
Or choosing to love life.
For what your thoughts and feelings are
Determines how conscious,
You are by far.

Knowing what you meditate upon,
You are!

The Brotherhood reminds us
Discordant feelings and thoughts produce
Disintegration, disease, old age,
And every other failure in the world,
Throughout all the ages.

He who cannot control his thoughts,
And feelings,
Will be left reeling
Throughout eternal oughts.

Mount Shasta Brothers, in closing
Wish us to also know
The first step to control self
Is to place all activity of mind and emotion
Upon the shelf.

32.
THE ASCENDED
STATE, MAN'S FATE

Those in the Ascended State
Can control the atomic structures
Like a sculptor with a slate.

Every electron and atom
Is obedient to their command
Because of their God Power stand
Of which they have earned the right
To have that mighty hand.

Mankind in the un-ascended state
Marvels at this fate,
But it is no more effort for them,
As when we act upon a whim.

The God-Self in us all
Can change human condition
So there is never a stall.

Every one of us has the Divine Flame
Within them, the same.

So as I awaken the sleeping
God-Self in me,
I dream of joining it, in the we.

33.
BE QUIET,
MY CHILD, FOR A WHILE

❦

INSPIRED BY ST. GERMAIN

It is essential that we quiet
Our emotions, body and thoughts
In order to transcend this frequency
Of our oughts.

Before going to sleep,
And in the morning before creeping about,
Become still, my child
And see yourself
Enveloped in a Dazzling White Light,
For a while.

Feel the connection
Between your outer and inner
Mighty Gold Self
Focusing upon your heart space
As a Golden Sun place.

Then accept with all your Right
The Mighty God-Presence
Of this Pure Christ Light.

Feel this great Light
Intensify in every cell of your body
And know you and it
Are no longer oddly.

Then, in closing declare:

We are Children of the Light,
We love the Light,
We can choose to serve the Light,
We live in the Light,
We are maintained and sustained by the Light,
We truly bless the Light.

Then, with all your might,
Know all this is truly right,
For we are what we think, all right.

34.
CAUSE AND EFFECT

There is a cosmic law
Called Cause and Effect
That automatically balances
In order to prevent a wreck.

This balancing process addresses,
And governs all forces everywhere
So we don't have to ever care.

If we understand this law,
We don't have to see human experiences
As wholly flawed.

This law is the only logical explanation
For the infinite complexities,
And experiences of many people and nations.

There really is no such thing
As chance or accident
That really never had
A true ring.

All is really under direct and,
Exact perfect law,
Where there can be no rawness.

For every experience
Has a former cosmic cause
Since everything is
The cause of a future eternal effect,
Thus, all can be correct.
Are we all set?

If you should injure one
Through one's life,
You are certain to know that form
In another life,
And endure that strife.

Through Cause and Effect
We can experience everything
Possible in the world
To know in effect
We are the same persona and thing.
Through freedom of choice and will,

We shall keep creating Cause and Effect
Till we know full well,
Our purpose is to,
Balance giving and receiving, female and male.

And then you'll really know
There is no such thing as we call
Hell.

35.
BRIGHT CHRIST LIGHT

Let the bright Light
Of the Christ Light,
Within,
Illuminate and purify
All radiating in and win,
So you may as simulate
The Plan of God,
Being Love, and Peace,
And Perfection for All The Good,
So your Divine Soul Plan, too, could, should,
And would...

36.
DIVINE DESIRE

Within every Divine Desire
Is the power of its inspire
Thus, creation.
We are the Children of Creation,
And through free will and choice
We can rejoice in our soul plan,
Knowing all desire directed
By the Divine within
Goes forth in love and blessings,
That know no end.

37.
NO MATTER HOW

No matter how strange, or impossible
An experience seems, not possible
To our present state of being,
It is no proof, dear one,
That there isn't a greater roof
Of wisdom and law
Acting to produce no flaw
In greater wonder of creation
Around us in relation, all the time.

38.
WHERE IS GRATITUDE

Beloved Children of blessed Earth
Arouse yourselves from the snare of five senses
That is most of your girth.

Awake from your lethargy
Before it comes much late
And face an un-welcomed fate.

Open your heart
To your unconscious emotions and thoughts
That creates your dualistic reality,
Having little or no thoughtfulness
Nor gratitude for your fortitude.

People O People, where is your gratitude
For Love of Life
That manifests your very multitude.

Oh how you often misuse and abuse
The energy of Life.

If it were not for
The Great Selfless Ones, Above and Below,
You would have destroyed yourselves
A long time ago!

39.
GOD'S BUILDING BLOCKS

What are the building blocks
That cause God to flock forward?
It is the transcendent and magnificent
Activities of Love and Light
That are the natural conditions of
God's creation of life, all right.

All in the universe lances
The Law of Love
Perfectly building and creating
Through love's perfect white light.

To live life through love
Is the Source of all life,
Preventing chaos' diced strife.

40.
FOREVER, LOVE

The Realms of Life
Are created by substance
So charge with Love
There can be neither imperfection nor discord,
There can only be afford.

This Perfection is ever active,
Ever expanding, ever blessing,
With Joy,
Forever more.

The human appetite and desires of self
Create emotions and thoughts
That often manifest nots.

If you so choose,
The time has come
To learn and apply
The Law of the Love.

You can keep choosing other
Till you may discover
Making another choice
To rejoice in the Law of Love.

Then you can release lack and limitation,
And separation,
Through consolation of the Law of Love.

Through the Center of your Heart
You will know
That Love is not an activity of mind,
But is the pure essence which
Creates the mind, all the time.

Love is Perfection manifest,
Only creating peace, Joy, and all the best.
It asks nothing for its self,
For it is a constant pouring out of self,
Being the Heartbeat of Heaven, To all else.

Oh, humanity only enough Love,
As you roam
Can truly bring you back Home!

41.
ETERNAL YOUTH?

Is there such a thing as eternal youth?
Is it really real?
Is so, how do we appeal,
To reveal it?
Let us see if we can unmask,
And move away the trash
In order to mix the recipe
To maintain and sustain
What remains, forever?

One Mighty Ascended Master
Has called eternal youth,
God's gift to Himself to His creation.

He goes on to explain,
Eternal youth is the flame of God
Abiding in the body of man,
Making him over, forever, more.

As we look closer at this youthful recipe

We see,
Eternal perfection can only be rightly achieved
By permanently casting out
All dense, negative light, in order to get it right.

There must be peace, love and light
Expressed in the outer self
For eternal youth and beauty
To be expressed as a Supreme Duty.

Youth, beauty and perfection
Are the attributes of
Love, which the God-Self
Is continually sustaining
And maintaining in its creation.

Through your emotions and thoughts
You can create vibrations
That shift your relations
Of self and others
Into a youthful formula,
Forming immortality.

For only feeling separate from self and Source,
Can you prevent eternal, youth and beauty,
Coming forth...

42.
ONE SOURCE OF ALL

SO SAYETH THE SAGE:

Life always has been,
Is now,
And always will be.

How can this be?

No one and no thing
Really can destroy life
As long as you choose to be one thing:
In tune with all there is of life.

Where doth all being originate?
Not in the doer but the beingness,
The Good-God seeingness in YOUR innate goodness.

The conscious acceptance of this truth
Will set you free
From the self-ruthlessness
Of non-free.

Through the constant use of God energy
You are guaranteed to maintain,
And sustain your energy of life.

At the end of your soul plan is a path
You will achieve,
Perfected mastery of your life,
And be relieved of any and all strife.

Then you will know
The full power of all,
The one source of it all,
All along was YOU!

43.
MASTERY MATTERS

What does it take to achieve Self-Mastery?
To have conscious control
Of all forces
And be able to manipulate all matter
The adept student blabbers.

The Master replies:
First, you must know your own God-Self, in the WE,
Second, have neutral feelings in all relations and
creations,
And third, be not able to misuse gained power,
through the ME.

For you are a star bound to a body,
And when you free WE from the ME
The star within you
Will shine bright for eternity!

44.
WHAT CREATED
OUR LIMITAITON

When man became sense conscious
Instead of Creator Conscious
A lack of conscious was created, then.

When hu-MAN-ity began to identify itself
With part of the Whole
Instead of the goal of the Whole,
A new imperfect role began.

Through freedom of choice and will
Mankind soon discovered
Limitation was the result of
The misuse of free will.
Man was now compelled to live
Within his own creation, until...

He soon remembers his noble birth
From the Great Source of All,
Then can choose to reconnect,
And recover from his great Fall.

45.
TRUE WEALTH

Man 'thinks' he controls his true wealth,
He hoards it, and keeps it even from self,
Keeping much more than he needs,
So others may not feed.

In his illusion man allows one percent
To control and withhold
Ninety-nine percent of the whole.

Only when man knows and understands
That the Great God-Self is the only
Real owner and controller of all wealth
Can he free himself from the me,
To consciousness of the we.

All wealth comes from the Earth, somehow,
And belongs to our Mother,
Who merely wishes that we share
With our sister and brother.

You have been shown
Who really governs the world's wealth?
Let this be the individual's soul test,
To see if you will and can share it with the rest...

46.
COMING OF JESUS

The coming of just Jesus
Was an uninvited invitation of Earth's people?
It was a karmic cosmic command
To use Divine Love, as equal.

The roaring and outpouring of this love,
Became the birth of the Christ love
In the people's unconditional love.

Jesus called forth a compassionate Cosmic Blueprint
For people to be treated equal,
And love one another,
No matter what the imprint.

Now we are awakening in the all-seeing,

The Christ Light within every human being...

47.
EGYPT

Egypt rose to her hefty heights
By the divine use of knowledge, power and light.
These attributes required,
Humility and obedience to the God Within
And unconditional control of the lower spin,
As the main goal.

When Egypt began her decline,
It was through the deliberate
Misuse of the incline;
Knowledge and power,
That created the darkest hour.

In her earlier epoch
Egypt produced great light,
And will soon have that sight, again...

48.
HOW TO CREATE

No form can come into creation,
Without a thought as a picture.
For every thought contains an idea
That is the criteria of expression.

Let us look at the process
That brings access
To creation...

What is it your wish to create?
Is it worthy of your time and energy?
What is your reason to bring this into existence?
Is it to satisfy an addiction or comfort zone
Or get you arrested on the way home?

Make sure what you wish to create
Has no motive or need to do harm to another,
But has an intention of a loving brother.

Write down your plan in your own words,
As clearly and consciously as you can,
Then you have a starting plan...

Know you have the ability to create,
See it like a picture on a plate,
The seeing and the power to create
Are the gifts of God-state within?

Seeing and feeling within yourself
Allows you to lift creation off the shelf.

The heart already knows,
But keep reminding the mind
Creation is the ability
To see the God within all the time.
For God is the doer, the doing, and the deed,
And you through Him can create, and proceed with,
Whatever you need.

Read your written plan again and again
At the beginning and end of each day.
This way your creation is downloaded in your heart
That is the best part and start.
Keep your intention to yourself,
Hold its power inside you,
So only you know its view.

When you are ready,
Steady yourself and allow

You inner vision to come through,
Consciously connecting to the Law of Making
And the God-within you to come fully come through...

Cast out all doubts and fear
And know in your heart
Your creation is near.

Have no set moment for results,
Just know you and God are issuing
The picturing of results,
With no wishing.

Allow yourself to be surprised and delighted,
And filled with gratitude
When your multitude, comes forth.

49.
SELF-MASTERY

See if you can never be surprised,
Nor taking things personally,
Nor not raised,
By the prize.

Dominion of self, at all times,
Allows the rhythm of life to manifest,
To rhyme.

Only by balancing of self
Can Self-Mastery be tested and bested,
Maintained and sustained,
Through no electricity but elasticity.

Be sure nothing from you is less than your best,
While not allowing a
Negative word or deed
To proceed.

All forces in the universe
Are waiting your command
Through the right use of tongue and hand.

The All-Controlling God-force
Lives deep within you,
Do not forget to use it and be true.

50.
WHEN I AM
AN ASCENDED MASTER

Someday when I am an Ascended Master, I AM
To graduate out of humanity
Into the full expression of my divinity.

Then I can break the barriers
Of lack and limitation,
And stand divinely free,
To be me,
Worthy to be trusted to embody
The forces beyond humanity's ability.

I shall then feel the Oneness
Of God's omnipresence,
Having all forces
Obey my command, at hand.

I shall be a Cosmic Conscious Being,
Being of free will,
Enrolling all my manipulation
Of the Light into my right site.

It is through the Light, adoring,
Through my Divine Love,
I shall go full exploring, for all.

51.
DIVINE ESSENCE

Divine Essence is the most sacred force
In the Universe.
It eliminates all discord
In order to afford perfection
In all direction.

Ascended Masters' bodies
Constantly cause the divine light out-pouring,
Loosening the mooring
To pale humanity's pouring of spite.

Through delicious Divine Essence,
The Masters of High are able
To care and protect
All on Earth's table.

Divine Essence,

Forever glows and goes
Like a spark,
One blows into a flame,
And ignites the dark.

52.
HIGHER BEING, NO MATTER

Beautiful Beings who Love and Support
The ever-evolving human space
Can be called Higher Beings,
Of Love, Light and Grace.

By bringing Forth
Their Love, Wisdom and Power
They deliver their God-Self,
Within each and every hour,
No matter.

They manifest their mastery,
Over all matter,
No matter.

Thus they've ascended into
The next dimension above
Human extension
To be divine,

All the time,
No matter.

The human race is often
Ignorant, or not believing
Of their great gifts,
Of giving and receiving,
Balancing rifts,
No matter.

But this does not matter,
For they keep spattering
Their eternal All Powerful Perfection,
No matter.

These Higher Beings
Truly have freed themselves
From human limitations,
And all evaluations
Through blazing outpouring of Light
That constantly brightens the night,
No matter.

53.
IF WE COULD SEE

If we could only see
How our own thoughts and emotions
Go out in the atmosphere
And create commotions.

Up in the ethers these
Emotions and thoughts go,
Gathering and gathering,
As they go,
Gathering more of their kind,
Each and every time.

For emotions and thoughts
Are powerful, pulsating things,
That bring,
More of their kind, and things,
Each and every time.

He who learns this lesson, well
Will apply the wisdom and control
To no longer allow thoughts and emotions
To run out-of-control,
Each and every time.

54.
EARTH'S CYCLE NOW

Planet Earth has entered
A most sacred cycle now,
Through ascension's,
Outpouring of great Light,
Somehow.

This is the grandest event
Earth and humanity have ever known,
To re-define and refine
All Love, and Light, with all our might,

For love and light
Are the future soul plan
Of our planetary home,
And us,
And also all other planets, and our sun,
A must.

All that does not come
Into perfect equality, harmony and balance,

Will not be the future life,
Of non-strife.

Know, Dear Ones, you have all gathered
Now for this blessed, amazing event
To begin and matter, right now.

55.
HOW TO CALL
A HIGHER BEING

To call a Higher Being
Let us first think upon them,
And in our mind's eye,
Let our seeing, become their being.

Call upon the Higher Being,
And they will answer every call
If your motive is for the good and love of all.

The Higher Being
Gives of itself unconditionally,
In all conditions, unceasingly.

Ask and ye shall receive,
If your intention is not to deceive.

For the Higher Being is here
Merely to truly please,
As you lovingly receive.

And when you meet a Higher Being,
You soon have a deep desire
To be who they are, just being.

56.
HOW TO RECEIVE YOUR GOOD

Universal Law teaches,
You cannot receive
What has not been earned,
And those are the terms.

Many feel they deserve,
And wish to attain,
This and that.
But exactly what are the terms
Needed for the deserved to be served?

If you so resonate,
Emboss in your eternal memory bank
What is about to postulate.
So you can finally tank
What you think you rank in your bank, account.

Your earning is manifested knowing
There is but one Source and Force
For all good.

And that is the interior God-Presence,
Living in your inside residence.

This Shimmering Self
Is the Life Force flowing and growing
Through everyone and everything
That enables the entire Universe
To sing...

57.
SOLAR SUBSTANCE

Solar Substance is in agreement
With your constant consciousness.
It is always responding
To your emotions and thoughts,
Whether you are aware of it, or not.

At all times we are given
This splendid substance,
Quantity and quality of self,
That reflects and creates
What we think and feel is real.

Humanity throughout the ages
Has misused this sublime substance
Through anger, confrontation and hate.

When these aspects of man
Are recorded in the heavens,
They create Earth's revengeful

Weather system to purify
The skies of hate.

Soon mankind will remember
How powerful they are,
And choose to use this creative substance,
Divine,
To clear and cleanse, body, soul,
And mind.

58.
WITHIN EACH OF US

Within each of us
Is the same power that can
Be expressed by higher beings
In any hour.

If you merely choose
To use this power of the hour.

Each human has a freedom of choice
To express their higher self,
Or something else.

You are the chooser
Of your own expression,
The Self-Conscious Creator
That no longer has to be the loser.

At any time you can choose
To rise above lack and limitation,
And any imitation of life.

Simply apply all your energy and determination
And you will achieve all your needs,
And succeed.

Now know, Dear Ones,
The God in you
Is always directing,
And perfecting
The Master inside you.
What do you choose?

59.
THE LONG JOURNEY HAS ENDED

The long journey for humanity
Is coming to an end.
The laws of cause and effect,
And learning what is through what is not,
Are finally ending and naught.

We have traveled as from the Light
As we could go,
Now it is time to turn around,
And face the glow.

To know our glorious selves
Glowing in the sight
Of the eternal ascended being
That is our divine right.

You are simply God's living temple.
That's all you need to know, it's that simple,
Now go and grow and expand

Into your divine soul plan.
The long journey is over,
You don't have to learn this way, again.
Let us join hands together,
And be One world family,
Once again.

60.
HIDDEN TREASURES #1

There have been many Golden Ages
Upon the plate of planet Earth.
Many are still hidden in ashes
Of time's passage.

Cosmic cataclysms of nature
Cleverly hide many treasures away,
So now at long last,
We may discuss and some discover, this day.

Remains are still in physical format,
For some.
But others still fully exist
In another dimension,
Oh, wow!

Whether in this dimension,
Or another,
These marvelous past cultures bring forth
Treasures of teachings
To support our next port.

The time has now come
To re-connect with our past,
Whether here or there,
Our Golden Age cometh, at last!

61.
THE POWER WITHIN

Throughout humanity's history
People have not understood
Life,
Thus, much strife has with stood.

People seem to drop into depression
Rather than understand how life
Can compress into compassion.

They seem not to know
Their blessings are the result
Of something within,
Rather than outside in.

It is an innate fantastic force
That's always been there.
It's just a matter of accepting it,
And bringing it to the fore.

All that we've experienced
Is meant to awaken this internal force,
And know we are the source within.

Through this Self-Source
We can know who we are,
And why we are here,
And then the real fun can begin.

Once we know the Source
We can choose to be in service to All,
And never have to fall, again.

Then forever more...
It's win, win, win, win, win.

62.

HIDDEN TREASURES #2

There is great wealth
And gold and treasure
Hidden in measure within the Inner Earth.

How does one access
The non-cash and the stash?

From Master's on high
We are told, no gold nor treasure
Can be distributed,
Until the surface-selfishness
Is not near.

Until things finally shift
It would be fast folly
To allow mankind to waste
Any more of nature's gifts.

But for the moment
Rest assured, be comforted in knowing,
There is a rescue treasure remedy
When we are ready
To fund our conscious growing.

63.
LOVE: LAW OF LIFE

We know the old adage,
Love Is All There Is.
Well, the ole Masters say it
This way: There is only One Law of Life,
And that is Love.

Love is the highest vibration in Creation,
Allowing all manifestation making.

Through man's thoughts, emotions and deeds
Man really never ceases
Creating his needs.

The absence of love
Is ever present,
Most often in fear, ever near.

That not of love
In effect becomes self-centered darkness

Moving in its own orbit,
Not allowing any love sparkness.

When the Law of Love is enforced
All negativity goes to sleep,
And we have no need to weep.

Through love the glorious God-Power
Within you awakens,
You release and express love
And there are no longer any hateful hours.

For you have allowed
The love-flowers, to bloom,
And there will be no further room
For anything other than what love can swing and
bring...

Love is the vibration and glue
That created everything,
Especially YOU.

64.
CHILDREN OF LIGHT

When we Children of Light,
Are ready to be adults,
And stand strong in our might,
Against the opinions of the world of ignorance,
Then we shall bear true witness,
To the marvels of the Manifestation of Light.

Great wonders wait us
Through the use of Light and Sound
When we shall be able to create
All about us, through a simple shout.

One suspicion or doubt
Of this truth will prevent you from
Bringing it out.

Trust and surrender,
To the unknown,
Is what it takes,

For not even one atom
Is allowed this mistake.

You are experiencing God's maternity,
So everything waits,
In order for you to morph into this thing
Called eternity.

65.
SOURCE OF ALL

Love is the very Hub of Creation,
All love aspects are spokes
Off the hub creating a Wheel of Creation,
Manifesting loving elation.

Love is the Heart,
The force, the Source of all.
Can we now hear the call of our Hearts?

In scientific terms,
Love expresses itself
As the force between the source of electrons,
So everything can run.

Through love's force
The electron is Pure Spirit
Or God's Light,
Unconditional Love, Perfect,
All ways right.

The word is made flesh
Through the mesh of God's love.

Sweet thoughts or compassionate feelings,
Are activities of love reelings,
Within the human mind and heart.

Whoever makes themselves
Fully available and sits at the table
Of The Law of Love
Is completely able to always stay at that table.

Through our free thoughts and feelings
We have the power
Within every hour
To sink to our lowest thought or feeling,
Or rise to the highest.

66.
HOW WE ARE MADE

Our individuated self
Often 'thinks' that
Its energy and power
Exists from itself.
Forgetting every aspect of self
Came from the God-Self.

Our mental body forgot
Even the atoms from our physical bodies
Are loaned by a force outside self.
Funny how the mind wants to take credit all the time.

Let us feel our hearts with gratitude
For the multitudes
Of everything given to us
From higher altitudes.

For in truth, every aspect of self
Is borrowed from the shelf
Of the Great Chef
Who mixed and made self.

67.
BALANCE OF
GIVING AND RECEIVING

The grand balance of life
Is maintained and sustained
By giving and receiving.

Here's the deal,
We cannot receive without giving,
And we cannot give without receiving,
In real.

How do you feel about this deal?
Does it seem real, in your life?

Many have been taught
It's better to give than receive
But this is a bit of a deceive.

If you don't receive in balance
Within what you give,

You soon lose the energy or desire to give.
Thus, no balance to live.

This bewitching balance
Is based upon loving self enough
Not to leave self-love on the shelf, of life.

To achieve this birthing balance,
We speak our truth,
Define our needs,
And set some boundaries,
In order to relieve, at lack of balance.

Do you know your truth?
Who you are and why you are here?
Do you know your needs?
Or are they stuck in the weeds, of life?
And last but not least,
Have you set boundaries in all relations?
So balance can bring full elations?

There are many rules and tools,
Once again revealed to man
To support you in knowing when, what and where
And how to stand,
Through who and why, in balance.
For without balance,
We fall off the soul plan beam,
And into the stream of imbalance,
And possible malice.

68.
PEACE AND HARMONY

There is a Magic Key in life
That unlocks and releases
The doors of all strife,
Through the Inner God-Power
That can be available
Each and every hour of your day.

The continual adoring and pouring
Of feelings of Peace and Harmony
To all humanity,
Eliminates calamity.

The essential intention of
Feeling Peace, Harmony and Serenity,
Will create ascended eternity.

Fortunate indeed are those
Who have mastered this truth.
Without it,
Humanity has no roof.

So we are speaking of
One of the nice Laws of Life,
In order to allow you to
Manifest Peace and Harmony.

69.
WONDERS
EXIST EVERYWHERE

There are seen and unseen worlds.
And whether you believe this or not, does not matter.
What matters is for you to know
Wonders exist everywhere,
Whether you know or believe it, or not.

Probabilities and possibilities
Live in the unknown
And when we can surrender to them
They become our own.

The Creator wishes to remind you,
All things are possible
Through knowing your divinity
Which is, by the way,
Always within your vicinity.

The more we embrace and love
Our divinity
The sooner the wonder appears from eternity
And becomes your certainty, for sure.

70.
ENDING WAR:
THE NEXT GOLDEN AGE

It is furious folly for one part
Of God's creation
To war against another part.

When will you know
War simply does not work!

Confrontation is the height
Of selfishness and lack of self-love,
Creating bondage and misery
Where there can be no peace of the dove.

Awaken weary world
And know
Soon you will bless your sisters and brothers,
Rather than wage wrongful war.

Learning what is
From what is not
Is done.

For the time of duality and separation
Is through
As you know the true you,
As Children of Earth
Sent here for preparation,
To now end duality and separation, forever more...

Now focus on creating your next Golden Age,
And remember,
You are destined to be
The Master Teachers and senders
Of Liquid White Light and Love,
Throughout the Universe,
In Oneness, for ages more...

71.

THESE THREE

❦

FROM MANY ANCIENT TEXTS, SENT ASUNDER:

(1) The most powerful and loving
Force is that which created us.
The greatest happiness
Comes from adoring and exploring
Your Source of ALL.

(2) The most eternal and real
Force is the I AM PRESENCE
Within each of us.
Stand true to the I AM
Within you.

(3) The most truthful force
Is The Light, as us.

Allow your Light
To eliminate your shadow
In the bright.

So be these three...

72.
WE IMMORTAL BEINGS

❧

We are all immortal beings,
Presently being in physical bodies.
Most are not aware of this state-of-being.

As a result of forgetting the truth
We have brought ourselves and planet
Near a ruthless disaster.

It is time to wake up,
And remember,
Who we are, and
Why we are here,
And lose the fear through not remembering.

Many extraordinary teachings and tools
Are coming to support
The new pivotal, precious Laws of Oneness,
That enables and enforces the rules of immortality.

Through discernment apply these rules
That necessitate,
So we may realign our priorities
And allow the creation of new sororities of equality,
harmony,
And truth that shall rule the world ever more.

73.
BEING PHYSICAL

In order to be fully physically formed,
We chose, it was required,
That we forget our
True Divine Essence and heritage,
So we could completely experience
All the 3D heredity.

This way we could learn
All there is to know
About what is,
Through what is not.

This lesson of learning,
Is complete,
And no longer has any yearning.

It is now time to command and demand,
That this forgetting veil
Be sent to jail,
And never seen again.

74.
LISTEN TO YOUR HEART

The mind believes,
The heart knows.

So how do we listen to
The knowing heart and start
To access the wisdom within?

We can begin,
By asking our soul
To let us into our heart,
So we can see our true part.

The soul knows darn well
And can make suggestions,
Of a personal process,
Answering questions, as a good start.

If we can only listen
We can ask our soul again
To reveal our true role

That has been hidden,
That we shall now rid the hidden.

Finally, we can ask the heart itself that knows
To show us exactly how we can
Grow and expand,
And create our True Soul Plan.

75.
QUEST FOR TRUTH

We are beginning to remember
Our Oneness with ALL THERE IS.
Life is a journey about self-empowerment and
realization,
Filled with our chosen teachings' revelations.

The bonds of untruth remain strong,
As we seek to eliminate the wrong.

Let us never abandon the quest for the truth,
For the truth will set us free
From you and from me.

Real truth, new truth is
Being revealed now.
If they resonate, apply them,
If not, deny them.

The new truths are waiting
Those who can accept them,
And let the old beliefs
Die like a whim in the wind.

76.
CHILDREN TODAY

Many teachings acknowledge the
Worth in being child-like.
But today, we have a new view
Of children being gifted,
Those who truly know,
How to show us the way...

Today, many children,
Indigos, Rainbows and Crystallines, too,
Have advanced cellular memories
To show us through
A doorway leading to a
New world paradigm,
Of equality, oneness and harmony,
So we no longer have to
Experience acrimony.

Pay attention to children's new ideas,
As they share,
Their suggestions and reflections,
Of a new world fair.

Children laugh and play
Because it is fun.
Ask them to teach you how it's done.

Parents please remember
To love and nurture,
Teach and support the young.

While they are temporarily in our care,
They will soon show us the way
Of being fair, and how it is done.

77.
CHANNELING HIGHER REALMS

The best way to connect and channel with higher
realms
Is to get yourself out of the way.
In fact, that is the only way
To receive a clear, concise message,
Not filled with your filter.

Begin by stating to yourself,
This is not about me,
I clear myself of myself,
In order to receive,
And be in service to the we.

Channeled information is best
Received by those
Who have chosen to arrest
Themselves in a personal process,
Clearing and releasing wounds,
Ego defenses, and the rest.

This allows a state of neutrality,
Moving me out of the way,
To be a good messenger
For myself and others
That day.

78.
PAST AND PRESENT

There was a time when
Love, Joy, transparency,
And authenticity existed
In all human transactions
And factions of life.

Humanity is in the process
Of returning to this state of being
So we don't have to be
The way we are,
Much longer.

For now, we are here
To bear witness,
To what we need to learn in order to be firm
In returning to our
Previous state of being.

This requires the full integration
Of our human and spiritual parts.
In order that we don't depart
From Unity Consciousness,
Moving from the me to the we...

79.
TRUTH LIVES

What the world now needs most
Is a good dose of truth?

To be untruthful has
Become a cultural norm,
And turned us into
A ruthless race.

LET US RETURN TO TRUE TRUTH NOW!

Truth lives in the hearts
Of all humanity.
Let us re-open our hearts
And reveal our loving parts,
Once more.

The truth that lives in our hearts,
Can be easily accessed
When we connect with our hearts.

Let us move beyond mental
Belief systems that close our hearts,
Creating lack, limitation, separation,
And aggravation.

Truth comes through love and oneness,
Not fear and control and aloneness.

The truth will set us free
To be we, and free
To be ourselves, and truly know,
The truth about you and me,
We are One, in truth.

80.
WISDOM

Be not proud of your wisdom,
Those who think you know it all.
For confidence is just an ego defense
Of the wounded child not feeling good at all,
Being left out on the fence.

Discourse with the ignorant and the wise,
For in reality, we are all simply teaching
What we need to learn, and prize.

If some looking shallow
Comes to you full of knowledge,
Listen and heed
For wisdom has no greed.

81.
A FRIEND

If you wish to know
Who a friend is,
Why he is here,

Do not ask his friends,
Spend time alone with him,
And ask him.

Converse like a whim in the wind,
Testing his heart,
By words, deeds, and actions
Which are the true factions,
Of a friend.

82.
WE ARE ONE

As soon as we can realize
We're a collection of soul connections
Then duality and separation
Will be simply sent, away...

We shall know we are surely
One old soul
Who has never really
Been sold into separation.

The vicious veil of separation
Is finally to be lifted.
We're being released,
From duality,
That never had any reality.

We are One Divine Soul,
Old in our role,
Of consciousness and love.

Every creation molecule,
Knows it's all been a silly ridicule,
Until now.

83.
STAR DUST

Humankind is but a Star
Bound to a body.

That's why you always knew
You are a Star, from a far.

We are literally made of star dust
That has kept us from rusting,
For eons.

What a great start,
Aren't we smart?

It is time to remember,
We are a member
Of a great Light.

When we know this for sure
We'll be freed from our physical form
To roam the cosmos, ever more.

Only through fully knowing
Where we came from
Can we know where we are going?
Allowing the Star Light
To keep us glowing and going...

84.
UNCONDITIONAL LOVE

Unconditional love is built
Around the concept;
The god within me acknowledges,
The god within you.
But few apply this moment to moment.
Do you?

True mother love comes close
To most of unconditional love,
Placing the we,
Before the me,
While honoring her truth, needs and boundaries,
Surrounding self.

Your soul truly exists,
And persists throughout eternity,
So there is time to learn
This lesson of non-provisional love.

We shall soon know
That trust of self and God
Are key,
To see me in the we,
To see beyond the weeds and me,
Into the we of unconditional love.

85.
A PERFECT PERSON

Inside each of you
Lives a perfect person,
Who knows exactly
The right thing to be and do,
During all actions.

This perfect person,
Knows full well
Right from wrong,
And how to be strong
In the right well come.

Your perfect person
Is ready to leave
Their comfort zone
Of Being wrong,
And assist someone
Who is not so strong?

When this happens,
Magic manifests,
And you can rest assured,
And know,
You've allowed someone else to grow.

86.
FEAR

The emotion of fear
Is most often ever so near,
It so appears.

Some say fear
Is an ear not hearing love,
Looking through the rear
View mirror of life.

We're not born with fear,
So how does it become so dear,
To so many?

It is carefully caught and taught,
And through it we,
Become completely distraught.

Fear based thinking
Closes our heart,
And makes it harder

To access others' emotional parts,
Of self.

So let's kill fear,
So it's never near again.

87.
THE UNKNOWN

When we surrender to the unknown
The entire universe
Of possibilities and probabilities,
Starts showing and growing,
Reversing adversity.

What we call the void,
Or nothing at all,
Is filled with electromagnetic
Forces of creation and consciousness
That is beginning to make sense.

The mind wants to know now,
To control and be the role maker,
But the heart knows things,
Are not what they seem,
For in the unseen,
Are many seeming's?

So trust and let go,
Surrender to not knowing,
Watch out for what starts,
Showing and growing, by not knowing.

88.
ALL ONE

In ALL space.
ALL things are One.
Though it seems divided,
Dualistic and separated,
It is only ONE.

ALL that exits,
Comes from the Light,
And that's ALL right.

ALL light comes,
Forth from the ALL,
Never being small.

ALL is,
ALL THERE IS.

89.
THROUGH THE HEART

Do you want to gain wisdom?
Seek it in your heart,
For your heart knows all,
No matter how large or small.

Do you want to gain knowledge?
Seek it in your heart,
For the mind believes,
And heart leaves belief,
And knows its part.

Do you want power?
In each and every hour
Seek it in your heart,
For the God-power within
Originates from your heart.

Now when you gain ALL
Through your heart,
Become one with your heart.

90.
TURNING IN

Turn your thoughts,
Inward,
Not outward,
To begin, my friend.

Find the Soul Light within,
Not outward,
My friend,
For only inward does the Light,
Through its wayward,
Shine inside out.

Know all self-masters,
My friend,
Reside from within,
Not without,
The end.

91.
CHILD OF THE STARS

Man is truly space born,
A son of the sun,
A sister of the Stars.

Our bodies are like comets
Shooting through space,
Racing to our destiny,
With our soul plans all in place.

Our minds are like planets
Thinking their way through
Life's pathway, never
Knowing the exact exit.

Our emotions are like moons,
Shining through the night,
Avoiding feelings with all our might.

All this is revolving around
A Central Sun,
Someday soon, we shall know,
It was all just meant to be fun.

92.
MERKABA

The merkaba is the way
To wed the spirit
To the body
So they don't oddly separate.

Everything in the universe
Has a merkaba,
In order to be unified and
Make-able and not break-able.

'Mer' means vehicle
In order to cycle things about.

'Ka' means light
So that things stay bright and right.

'Ba' means body
So we have something to contain,
And maintain and sustain it all.

Blessed is the marvelous, macambo merkaba,
For dancing all about,
And making all things amazingly plausible.

93.
IS TIME ALL THE TIME?

Time changes not,
But all things change within time,
Yours and mine.

Time seems to be a force that holds
Events in separation and isolation.

Time is not in motion,
That's just a notion,
So why all the commotion about time?
But you move through time
Time and after,
As consciousness moves through rhyme,
Like one event to another in a flutter.

Parallel to time,
There exists ALL THERE IS.
Know that, as you might feel separate in time,
You cannot be other than one with
Time, all the time.

94.
A MAGIC CHAIR

Legend tells of a magic chair,
Out there that can transport
Us from here to there, everywhere.

It's a magic chair
That soon will come from there
To here to move us through air and everywhere
To an amazing new way of being and seeing.

It will assist in rising
Physical form components into
Its divine purity and structure, raising
The electronic body into bliss,
By seating and going through the mist.

Here's the reveal, once perfected,
The perfect body remains
Forever eternal youthful,

Beautiful and strong.
Wouldn't you like to have this deal,
And not have it go wrong.

In this new body
You can do anything
Wherever you choose in the universe,
With no adverse reactions,
Anytime.

Then there will be no barriers of time place,
Nor space or condition of being.
In freeing self of every conceivable
Lack and limitation in any station,
Of being.

The desire for this perfection
Exists and is an innate idea
Within many civilizations.

In many legends and myths
Of almost every race and nation
There exist stories of being
Immortal perfected beings,
Always being beautiful
From ageless age to age.
Suppose we were to tell you
This is the master blueprint

Upon which humanity was imprinted,
Eons, ago.

And that this magic chair really exists,
Right now,
And will soon persist...

95.
LAW OF LOVE

When humanity finally finds the fortitude
To live with the everlasting Law of Love
We shall discover the release
From the cycle of birth and rebirth.
This will surely bring much mirth.

The reason and existence of humanity
Is to learn to love
Self, thus others, unconditionally.

Once this is finally in place,
The perpetual problems of the human race,
Will finally erase.

In problem's place will be
Ever expanding joy and truth
That forever creates fruitful youth.

With no blockages,
We shall then dock at

Constant new creations of what
Abides and builds in love.

Life is perpetual perfect motion
That neither sleeps nor slumbers,
And love is the sustaining stream
That means continuous creation.

When we succor self and are obedient
To the Laws of Love
The last enemy of man will be arrested,
Death will disappear,
And be dissolved in ever lasting
Life of love.

96.
OUR HIGHEST SELF

✿

The highest aspects of ourselves
Do not recognize and can never
Create through the confines of confusion,
And chaos that exists in our lower
Mental body, so oddly.

If the individuated self
Does not call the
Power of Presence into
Action there can be no satisfaction.

There will only be outer experience
That reflects the ever-changing conditions,
Or junk yard mine fields of our feelings and thoughts
Surrounding all the oughts.

Our higher selves abides and rides
Within our electronic body,
Towering high above us,

And is concerned only in creating,
And expanding beyond us.

Only in transcending Earthly laws
Do we claim our God-given
Power and hour to live and
Create without any flaws.

This power is changeless perfection
That knows no defection,
Expanding, forever more.

97.
WHEN WE SAY, I AM

When we say I AM
We are being the creative
Consciousness of our God-being, seeing,
And announcing, and creating, the being
Of creation, at a particular spot in the universe.

The being is the only energy
In existence whose nature
Is to manifest in some manner,
Being I AM.

Then we are being the Law of Being,
And no one and no-thing,
Can change our seeing.

For life is the only
Presence,
Knowing and power,
That can and will act in every hour.

Every one of us can be perfection,
At every intersection of life.
It takes no more energy,
To be perfection,
Than the correction, of life.

98.
DIVINE LOVE

Divine love contains perfect activity
In every sacred second of the God-within.
When we enter the conscious path
To Self-Mastery, we understand and know,
We declare, we demonstrate
Divine love from now on...

For divine love contains
Wonder-filled wisdom and perfect power.
It is composed of wondrous wisdom
And all-ready power of the God hour.

When we manifest enough divine love,
And send it out,
We demand and command the love,
All around.

So love your divine love,
Immensely and then,
Nothing else can enter mentally, but love.

99.
ASCENDED
MASTERS, AMONGST US

Ascended masters are always amongst us,
Guardians and gifts of humanity,
Who have worked many millennia
From the unseen to the seen

They enlighten and brighten and lift
Humanity out of our self-created
Self-centered creations.

These higher beings' domain
Is beyond death's doors,
Having eternal dominance
Over the physical body and terrain.

All things obey their command,
As they demand the laws of nature,
And the universe is at their converse.

100.
LIGHT DEFINED

Light is matter, energy and luminosity,
One in all three,
So you can see light.
That makes up, and wakes up
The eternal spiritual body, all right.

This immortal light body is
Composed and condenses,
In a sense,
By your I AM Presence, in residence,
Which is self-maintaining and sustaining,
Ever expanding, ever perfect purpose,
And the catchall of divine light,
Truth and Power
From the very heart-center of creation.

This white light body,
Is your eternal, individuated
Lyre of life, and heartfelt center
Of manifested form.

In its present form,
We can only behold, not hold this holy form,
Not even for a half-second of a second.

But someday soon, if we so choose,
We shall ascend into,
This white body of light,
And leave never more.

101.
TWIN FLAMES, EXPLAINED

Twin flames are from the
Same divine flame,
Almost the same.
These flames, not exactly the same,
Come from the Center of Creation,
The conceptor of Universal Consciousness,
Not always amongst us.

Our first individuated form is
Through the formation of a flame,
Does that help explain.
Your individualized presence?

Since light is the basic component,
Or energy, of which all forms are formed,
It makes sense that this is where the flame is born.

When you connect with the
Reflected divine aspect of self,

You have met your twin flame,
And things will never be the same, again.

For together you may choose
To lose all human parts
That could ever keep you a part.

Never a part you will then start
To connect with ALL THERE IS,
And define and refine,
Your true mission and begin.
To control all manifestations,
As a part of your start.

102.
PAIN OR PEACE, EXPLAINED

Through freedom of choice and will
Each of us given the free flexibility
To think, feel and create any experience,
Through free will, incredibly.

If we choose to use energy,
And our beingness positively,
We can create peace,
Peacefully.

If we choose to think and feel negativity,
We thrust imbalances and unwanted boundaries
Into ourselves, and we create pain,
Painfully.

Through OWNERSHIP and taking
Responsibility for being
The Creator of our lives,
We can make new choices,
To allow,

The highest expression of self,
To take place,
Peacefully.

After we've had enough pain,
Maybe we can realize
Peace is an easier path,
At last.

103.
TRUE DESIRE, A MUST

Please trust and know
A must in being a higher being,
Attaining mastery over human high jinks
Thus gaining ascension,
Is achieved through deep divine desire,
The God-in-faction, in action.

The direction of divine desire is the,
Marvelous movement,
Ever expanding the locomotion of life, itself,
Whose motion can never be stopped?

But use your resonance and discernment
To discriminate between true desire,
And human haunting hunger,
For they are as far apart,
As lust and love, amongst us.

Human hunger is fed by habit,
And the five senses,

While divine desire is like a gentle rabbit,
Hopping along life expressing no bad habit.

Be holy honest with yourself,
For your motive to manipulate or manifest,
Only those things of pure thought and emotion,
Can prevent the commotion of life.

Remember whatever negative
Thoughts and emotions are sent forth,
They must first resonate within you,
In full view,
Before they are transmitted further,
Into the world.

Once out in the world,
There is a bit of a twist and turn,
As your thoughts and emotions
Gather more steam and their kind,
They turn back on you in like kind!

And this becomes the composite of
Your concern and consciousness.

104.
MAGIC MIRROR

There is a magic mirror,
That really exists.
When we have reached a certain position in our
personal process,
It persists in showing us pictures
Of our past and present lives.
Showing our evolutionary position and pictures of
our progress.

You stand in front of this magnificent glass,
And pitch your soul's light into it,
Hold it there with all your might,
And look upon the reveal, which is real.

Life after life appears,
Some in serious successful detail,
Others where you de-railed your life,
Through strife and struggle.
But through it all,
You grew and expanded,

To witness the perfect presence,
Of you.

When you become worn out and weary,
Of these ways of burning out your learning.
Then you begin earning,
Your way back into bliss.

You finally see in this magic mirror
A perfected version of you,
Shining ever bright, through the new dew of you,
Not having to learn what is,
Through what is not.

105.
SERVICE

What does it mean to be
In true service to another?

What we think is service to all,
May not be service a' tall.

What many people consider service
Is mostly loss of self in others.
The act of satisfying and gratifying
The limitations of self,
Is not service.

This is the denigration of spirit,
And a dramatic demonstration of our
Lack and limitation.

The first and true service of anyone
Is the love and support of
The God-force within you,

The great master servant of self,
And teacher of everyone.

During our service to another,
If we hold our attention other than on
The Inner Source and Force Within,
We shall never win,
We shall move from servant to slave.

For when we possess this Inner-Force,
We can fully serve another,
Through having served self first.

For true service can only come
By embracing the master within,
That allows us to balance,
Giving and receiving, out and in.

Let us beware that our service to others,
Is not an excuse,
To strut our stuff,
In the presence of others.

106.
FEAR

It seems fear is everywhere.
But what is the purpose of fear.
It appears to be one of the main emotions
Of mankind,
Not being so kind.

Fear is the wide-open mouth
Of the monster-of-man that
Can control and create
Feelings of hate with disastrous dealings.

Some say fear is the absence of love,
That imbalances the ideas of mankind,
Through its non-abstinence.

There is a fabulous flame that can
Tame fear.
It is called the Violet Flame,
That can extend from head to toe,
So you know there is nothing to fear,

Putting the flame near,
Your fear is placed in the rear of your life.

Focus on this flame,
Nothing will ever be the same.
It clears and cleanses all
Impure thoughts and emotions,
That cause all commotions.

Ask this voluptuous violet light to
Raise and blaze through you,
So you have a new view of life.

Then it will take away negative emotions and thoughts
From you,
Ending all cause and effect,
Past, present or future
And replace all the flameless oughts
With the fullness of you.

For fear is an illusion,
That was just here to confuse you.

107.
PAST LIVES

If we could only remember,
And understand that
Repeated Earth lives
Are an optimistic opportunity
To take ownership, correct and balance
Mistakes of past lives,
Becoming a true member of life.

Then we just might
Use every experience
To make a legal contract with learning,
Instead of resisting,
All we create,
Not seeing ourselves as victims,
Always persisting.

When we finally become conscious,
Of the purpose of past lives,
Learning the lessons of each one,

Then we can leave the
Rotating wheel of incarnations,
Through free will,
And become immortal, at last.

108.
LIGHT

Light itself cannot be nor,
Receive imbalances within itself.
For Light is all perfection.

To create imbalance it comes
From the personality of humankind
With thoughts and emotions,
Not in balance, imperfection.

Imbalance can be balanced,
Through acceptance and compassion,
Creating forgiveness and,
Universal Love, as a passion.

When forgiveness is true,
It is Light filling,
Everything and everyone,
Bringing Light's Perfection,
Into all direction.

It's impossible for your life
To be right or anything other than what
You bring to it,
So why not the Light.

109.
MOTHER TAKES A BATH

It's no secret how much
Mankind has abused and
Misused Mother Earth.

We rape her body, so oddly,
By taking her vital organs,
Air, water, oil and minerals,
Like there is an endless supply,
Not thinking or caring we are killing
The Mother whose body,
We so rely.

The time has come for Mother Earth
To protect and serve herself,
Due to the lack of consciousness,
Among us.

All nature is a self-purifying and protecting,
Let us now stop

Mankind's endless capacity for destruction,
So new constructions can begin.

Mother Earth's method of self-defense,
Is to return to humanity her offense.
That which has been imposed upon her,
For eons past, that shall no longer last.
So mankind shall now experience
Universal Law:
What you cause others to experience,
You shall experience yourself,
In the end.

When mankind, not being kind,
Has fully awakened and gained further wisdom,
We may join in perfect cooperation
With the magnificent force of Mother Earth,
Creating heaven on Earth,
Being One again.

110.
LABOR OF OUR LOVE

The greatest power in every hour,
Ever at hand,
For ourselves and our use,
Is the labor of our love
As an energy like a finger pushing through a glove,
Resolving and solving,
All human dilemmas
That perpetuates the human fondness for drama.

True love has no boundary,
Ever-flowing through wisdom,
As its domain.
It is the lifter of life,
And the pocket book of humanity.

When we stay connected to love,
All achievements and accomplishments flow,
And struggles vanish, and go,
As love becomes varnish vocalized.

When we adore love,
Loving results absolutely follow,
As we deepen our love of our fellow man.

The more we are being love and contemplating love,
The less we separate and isolate,
With people, places and things,
And your soul sings like a swinging swing.

III.

STATUE OF LIBERTY

What is the meaning of the
Stupendous Statue of Liberty
The goddess gracing New York harbor?
Her real purpose seems hidden,
In mystery and lost history.

She is a feminine focus of Spiritual Power
Guarding America each and every hour.
Her golden torch, held high,
Embodies the Light of the Mighty I AM PRESENCE,
Sending rays of love and peace,
To all Earth's residence.

The majesty and magic of her
Towering physical presence represents
The God-force within all of us,
Armoring America, and all beyond.

North America has Lady Liberty,
Holding the Christ-Light high.

South America has the Christ statue
Held high in the Southern hemisphere,
Both appearing mighty high.

It is not accident or chance that both
North and South hold the Christ-Light,
High, showing what both continents
Are willing to share with the rest of
The continuous world.

112.
THE SUN

The Sun of our Solar System
Is to the whole universal system
What our heart is to the human body.

The sun's rays of energy
Are the blood-stream system
Of this world, and beyond, it seems.

The lungs of Earth
Is the girth of the atmosphere,
Surrounding the planet,
Through which the effects of Sun's energy,
Constantly flow,
Clearing and cleansing the Earth,
As they go.

In addition to our heart,
The Sun is also our head,
The Father of the Family, if you will,
Of this entire family system,

Conducting the eternal energy,
Through freedom of will.

Want a shock; the sun is not hot,
As we think.
It's cool as a summer cucumber,
Gentle as an afternoon slumber.
It only needs to get hot,
When it passes through the gases
And near Earth's atmosphere.

Then Sun's energy becomes the electronic
Hold and pole of the Earth's magnetic poles,
And then the Mind of God,
Unites with the Soul of the Earth.

This is why we are the Suns/Sons of God,
Similar to the Sun,
Being one.

113.
GIVING THANKS,
HAVING GRATITUDE

We often focus on what is not,
Rather than what is,
In our lives.
Maybe it's time to turn the not,
Into thanks and gratitude for the what.

Most of us live life after life
Without once thanking or sending
Gratitude, and never mind love,
To the Divine Fantastic Forces,
Which flow through us, all the time.

When and where do we give regular thanks,
For the thousands of good things
Surrounding us all the time.
For the Godly-forces that created this good,
Who don't even ask anything in could or should.

Many even shame life,
Even hold a grudge,
And won't budge,
From blaming life,
For woulds or coulds, or shoulds,
They created themselves.

Let us fill our hearts with
Gratitude and offer a multitude
Of thanks for every single person, place or thing,
We create, and make possible,
The good and grungy,
Without any further platitudes,
Of non-thanks.

114.
WHEN MANKIND
BECOMES...

There is so much waiting
From higher realms to be given,
To humanity when we are ready,
And steady enough to receive it.

These new truths and wisdoms
Will change our lives for the better
Whether we know it now or not.
When we have the credentials,
The essentials will be revealed.

When mankind stops generating,
And creating destruction throughout
The land, we shall land in a new paradigm,
That will swell into heaven.

Through our disastrous feelings and thoughts,
Spread to the seen and unseen worlds,

Our intense vibrations are placed in many places and
spaces.
They hook themselves to humanity,
And we create insanity, again and again.

Humanity seems to have no understanding
Of what happens when we send
Our hateful stuff out into the rough.
Of life.

The feeling aspect of us is feminine,
From the activity of our heart space.
The thought side is masculine,
From the activity of our mental body.
Let us now allow the male and female to balance,
As the mind returns into service to heart,
So we never have to part again.

115.
THE WONDERFUL WHEEL

There is a Wonderful Wheel of wonderment
Which affects the welfare of the whole world.

It activates the direction of Light,
Within the sustained systems to which
We exit and persist.

When that wheel wanders into
The Way of Humanity,
And is nearer than we are aware of,
The wheel releases rays of light,
Upon the world,
And all our resistance to the light
Clears in sheer delight.

When we become spokes on
That great wheel,

That radiate out,
It creates a rotation,
That will allow no doubt.

Then we remember we are the Light.

116.
AS ABOVE, SO BELOW

Look above, or below,
Whether you can see it or not,
Things are the same.
It's all part of the Oneness
That is the essence of the Oneness and Same,
Game.

Whether high or low consciousness
We're all on the same path
And shall arrive at the same destination,
No matter the math.

There are forces above and below,
A plenty,
Sending wisdoms and love
To, we, in the middle,
Who have thought ourselves so little,
So long.

The time has come for the middle,
Above, below and not so little,
To join in the middle,
Once more.

Once we unite,
Things are going to get quite bright,
As legions of light and angels,
Dance with us in the middle, not so little.

When we unite with the bright light,
Our world service, and beyond
Begins and we shall experience
How truly mighty and grand our Soul plan,
Is.

Then, the 'is' joins the I AM,
And we know I AM is who
I AM that I AM.

PART TWO

MYSTICAL MESSAGES

Lemurian Council of Twelve Speaks

Introduction for Lemurian Messages

For some what is about to be said is a new truth, for others a myth, but whether you know or believe what is about to be said, what is asked of you is to focus on the message if you cannot accept the source. For those who know this is truth, enjoy the intended wisdoms.

There is no place in the universe where compassionate conscious beings may not go to explore and understand all cosmic creation and themselves. There is neither place nor condition that we may not go, explore, and understand, if we so choose. Lack and limitation are illusions of our lives that are now ending.

The idea that the center of the Earth is a mass of fire is not completely accurate. Within the crust of the Earth, for a certain depth, there are conditions of heat and molten rock acting, but within the center of the Earth itself there are conscious, higher frequency individual beings who, through many cycles of evolution and personal processing, have mastered the control of certain forces to accomplish the fulfillment of their divine soul plans for the interior of the Earth.

Only ignorance and lack of trust and enough light allow humanity to believe anything is impossible. The students of self-mastery and the cosmos truly accept A

Mighty Source of Creation, and what reasoning mind can doubt they know the Creators of Creation are all about, facing us everywhere on our planet without limit, loving and extraordinary.

Humanity is in the process of learning there is more in the universe besides itself, and the following Inner Earth messages contain part of that new knowledge for many and a reconfirmation for others. Storms may shut off the sun's light for a brief time, but they never will be able to shut the light out completely. One day the light will break through those storms, and that form is here now. Facts will be revealed that send unknowing away to be replaced by knowing great, new truths that will delight and not frighten you.

A while back I wrote a book called *Coming Home To Lemuria: An Ascension Adventure Story*; please allow these messages to be an addendum and concise continuation of teachings and messages from beings who love us more than we love ourselves.

Lemurian Council Message #1:

LEMURIA

There once was the Land of Lemuria
That stood in grandeur for millennia.
Some say it was fable,
While others knew it was quite stable.

The world now is really unstable,
As the old 'me' paradigm is dying.
The new 'we' world is trying
To create like the late fable,
Which was actually quite able.

Much of our reality is actually based on fable,
And it's time to know we are able to create new truths,
In order to allow humanity to create a new proof
Of where and when it all began
And why we are able.

Whether you believe it or not,
We are all from Lemuria's lot,
A land of light, which fathered divine, ought.

The time has come to journey home...
Now, that we have completed our arduous roam.

We have created all possible ways to separate,
And the time has come to truly patriate

Our Love and Light.

Let us linger no more,
As we heal our great sore.
The wisdoms that made Lemuria great
Are once again rising from tectonic plate.

Soon humanity will have available all the tools,
And know the rules to return to the light.

In great detail Lemuria is once again revealing
The right way back into the Light...

So with all your heart and might,
Are you ready to once again
Know we are The Beings of The Light?.

Lemurian Council Message #2:

DEAR BELOVED LEMURIAN DESCENDANTS:

Lemuria is often called the Motherland, the Father of humanity, and 'seeded' the evolution of human development. Lemurians came to this planet from another galaxy on a divine mission.

The Lemurians were some of the original civilizations to embody in advanced physical format what now is known as Homo sapiens. Other 'colonists' arrived elsewhere on the planet.

The planet was and is to be a divine experimental laboratory for the universe, a bringing together of as much diversity as possible.

You are still attempting to learn how to see yourselves as a diversified version of Oneness: the purpose of your planet.

Please allow this to begin a dialogue of where you came from, why you are here, and where you are headed...

- Phillip, with The Lemurian Council of 12.

Lemurian Council Message #3:

LEMURIA LIFE

Early in the Lemurian civilization when the
Lemurians experienced living within a dense,
physical body, it became obvious that in order to
stay connected to ALL THERE IS and create an
advanced civilization, their makeup would have to be a
combination of physical body and spirit. And the spirit
component would become the essential blueprint.

The higher realms' connections, where we all come
from and return, would allow the necessary access to
our true home of equality, harmony, and balance.

This spirit aspect would also allow souls to explore
other dimensions throughout the universe in order to
constantly grow and expand. A major benefit of staying
connected to spirit is that you always know who you
are and why you are here: a process we in 3-D are still
examining. Later we shall examine how the Lemurians
stayed attached and conscious of their spiritual
essence... A path for us now...

- Phillip, with The Lemurian Council of 12.

Lemurian Council Message #4:

HOW TO STAY CONNECTED TO SPIRIT

Early in the development of 'we,' human beings were not as dense as we are now; there was a 'lighter' connection to the planet, if you will. Thus, we Lemurians could choose a looser combination of dense body and spirit, unlike you today. In fact, the physical body was secondary to the higher vibrational spiritual/light body as primary, housing the physical.

We preferred the higher frequency, realizing all of Creation consists of various frequencies of energy. This allowed us to remain in contact with ALL THERE IS. We could travel in our light bodies to other dimensions and galaxies throughout the universe. This allowed us to gain great knowledge, talents, and tools upon which to build our advanced civilization.

Through your Ascension process, now you are remembering and recapturing this ability. This will also allow the union of our frequencies so that we may know we are one.

- Phillip with The Lemurian Council of 12.

Lemurian Council Message #5:

WE ARE ALL LEMURIANS

Downloaded within your DNA/RNA is all the
unconditional love and wisdom of Lemuria, which is
being activated during your ascension process now. You
are simply remembering your roots. Deep within the
eyes of your heart you know this. Open your heart eyes
and see us; feel the true you.

Allow yourself to now heal your wounds and ego
defenses and know we are all connected to each other
and the universe. All you have to be and do is trust
what you already have and know inside you.

Our genetic coding is the same: we are one. It's time
to unite and return home in oneness. ALL THERE IS
awaits you. Are you ready to receive it?

- Phillip with The Lemurian Council of 12.

Lemurian Council Message #6:

VENUS, THE PLANET OF LOVE, OUR ORIGINAL HOME

Before the advanced civilization of Lemuria came to planet Earth, we had a long evolutionary process on our sister planet Venus, the planet of love. We created physical formats that adapted to the gaseous environment of Venus. So, in reality, within our light/soul bodies, we traveled from our home galaxy and planet of Lemur to Venus and then migrated to Earth. In the less dense states on Venus, we were literally able to merge as One, embracing unconditional love. This love was transferred to the core of Earth in preparation for our later arrival there. Your ascension process on Earth now is activating this love from the inside out...

The time eventually came when we were to experience a denser physical form/existence and leave Venus and migrate to Earth, allowing the unconditional love within the Earth's core to guide us. Soon we were able to locate and inhabit the huge continent of Lemuria. We came to Earth to not only learn what we needed to learn from being more physically human, but to love and support through our vast knowledge all the beings on the planet and to know we are all connected, all one, and expressions of the same Source.

- Phillip, with The Lemurian Council of 12.

Lemurian Council Message #7:

THE DELAY

When the Christ walked the Earth some 2000+ years ago, there were several years that he seemed to have disappeared before returning to his teachings.

In addition to adept teachings in Egypt and Tibet during this period, he went into the Inner Earth and met with Gaia, Mother Earth. He asked for a 2000-year delay in her need to shift her axis—something each planet needs to periodically do. She granted it, and that time line has now arrived: this is the end of the Mayan calendar, not the end of the Earth.

- Phillip, with The Lemurian Council of 12.

Lemurian Council Message #8:

WHAT DID/DO WE LOOK LIKE? WHAT MADE US DIFFERENT FROM YOU?

As has been reported from many sources throughout time, Lemurians were/are tall, rather slender, and have a balance of the masculine and feminine energies, leaning more toward feminine in appearance and demeanor.

As has also been discussed in earlier dialogues, while Lemurians had physical bodies, they were not as dense as humans now. In fact, the entire Earth was less dense in times past. This is the reason there are so few physical remains of many past advanced civilizations. We often lived outside our physical bodies in etheric or soul/light bodies.

The entire molecular structure was loosely spaced in our light bodies, which created a beautiful glowing resonance. This structure allowed us to have the ability to move between multiple dimensions, as we stayed attached to our Earth bodies through a silver cord. This ability allowed us to fully connect with Universal Laws of Oneness and truth at all times. You, our brothers and sisters, are regaining this ability through your ascension process now. You are realizing you are multidimensional beings living in several frequencies at the same time.

- Phillip, with The Lemurian Council of 12

Lemurian Council Message #9:

LIGHT TEMPLES

The Lemurian civilization was maintained and sustained by a network of "light temples" that were connected to the universe, Inner Earth, and one another. Using sacred geometry and their network connection, the temples were built at energy vortices, which were "frequency portals" that supported the Lemurians' very existence and consciousness.

These temples allowed an ever-growing and expanding learning process through maintaining the important connection to Source; constantly healing/balancing the emotional, mental, and physical bodies; allowing astral travel around Earth, other planets, galaxies, and star systems; and supporting telepathic ability.

You are in the process of relocating certain temple vortices on Earth and recapturing the abilities associated with them...

- Phillip, with The Lemurian Council of 12.

Lemurian Council Message #10:

WAS LEMURIA THE GARDEN OF EDEN?

Some say Lemuria was the basis of the myth/story of The Garden of Eden. Well, whether it was or not, it was certainly like the fable of old.

Days were spent with perfect weather created by awakened consciousness filled with spiritual, creative, and joyful abundance. There was a love of beauty beyond your comprehension now that was expressed in our physical bodies and environment. Everyone's soul essence was honored, and we knew abundance through gratitude and balance came from our connection to ALL THERE IS. Our self-empowerment came from knowing and living our true soul plan.

Because there was no true separation from physical and light bodies, there was no separation of emotions or thoughts. There was an integration of all things through telepathy. Since you knew what others were thinking, it eliminated deceit and the denial of deceit. We were clairvoyant, and we all honored the Universal Laws of Oneness. ALL THERE IS energy was combined in all our existence. We practiced unconditional love knowing when we interacted with another we were in the presence of our mutual divinity.

Now knowing all these wonderful things about Lemuria you may ask how did we come to lose it? What caused it? And how can you prevent it from happening again when you achieve what we did? This is the great lesson for humanity at this time. There have been Golden Ages on your planet that have come and gone. Now you are being given the opportunity to create a final Golden Age that will not—cannot—end so you may go out into the universe and be the master teachers you are intended to be.

We chose to leave and shift to a higher frequency of existence due to the imbalance of the assertive masculine energy (Atlantis) against we, the Lemurian receptive feminine energy. You are now being giving the opportunity to finally balance these two forces of giving and receiving so you can create an entire world of equality, harmony, and balance—a worldwide "we consciousness of oneness."

Do you choose to now create a true Garden of Eden and join our civilization in the higher realms or stay in separation and confrontation?

Your Mother Earth has made her decision; all within and upon her body will be of a higher frequency or they will not be here. If you choose not to shift, you will continue your dense path elsewhere, knowing someday we shall all arrive at the same destination...what do you choose?

- Phillip, with The Lemurian Council of 12.

Lemurian Council Message #11:

CAN CRYSTALS COMMUNICATE?

Lemurian culture was/is extremely connected to Earth's nature. All of the elementals of nature—minerals, trees, air, water, fire, etc.—were/are essential aspects of our awareness and knowing. We can manifest crystals through our molecular, telepathic abilities and often found them existing throughout our large continent. Their various colors and shapes determined their use; this is a science unto itself and could fill many pages of many books.

We basically used crystals as energy connectors of giving and receiving. Your first radios were called "crystal sets." Crystals emit and receive energy, a balance of giving and receiving. Crystals were our 'mineral friends' who were used to heal our bodies and power our civilization. We knew/know they are conscious living beings. Through our light crystalline bodies, crystals enhanced our ability to remain telepathic and to stay connected and travel throughout the universe.

Much of your current technology is based upon crystal power and use. You will soon discover another higher purpose of these elements, which are the nervous system of Mother Earth, that can and will change your world forever!

- Phillip, with The Lemurian Council of 12.

Lemurian Council Message #12:

WHAT'S LOVE GOT TO DO WITH IT?

You have all heard much about love throughout the ages. That it is the building block of all creation: that love is the only real emotion and every other emotion is the absence of it, etc.

Since we Lemurians were connected to one another and the universe in a fundamental way, we had/have another level of experience within love. It was/is without resistance of any kind and a natural part of our being. Loving one another was/is the same as loving self since we know we are all one. You are still discovering/remembering this, Dear Ones. Once you assimilate this truth, your entire world will shift...

Our love was/is what you would call unconditional love (I see the god force within you that you see in me). It was not based upon loneliness, need, nor control. It was/is based upon "we consciousness" unity— something else you are in the process of learning.

We were/are openly affectionate with one another with no signs of taught shame or blame—sort of like you hippie lovers of the 1960s. In fact that 'movement' was a reconnection with our love. As then, our cultural, personal, and sexual relationships would appear very open and liberal to your taught ideas about intimacy

now. We had/have not religions or government barriers to our loving: it was divinely heartfelt. Even the Atlanteans were not understanding of our relationship with love.

There was no separation, duality, nor confrontation between male, female, racial, homosexual, or otherwise. This is something else you are learning not to be. Since love was an expression of our united divinity, it was/is embraced by all.

Since we did not kill one another or other living beings on the planet and remained connected to Creation, our lives were/are filled with trust and joy. In your future the need to kill will vanish in a flash of light.

Someday soon you will rediscover your divine love aspect of yourselves and know you are divine, loving beings of god, and any reflection of that is perfect.

- Phillip, with The Lemurian Council of 12.

Lemurian Council Message #13:

SO YOU THINK YOU'RE HAVING SEX

After our last Message #12: WHAT'S LOVE GOT TO
DO WITH IT, we felt your resonance to know more
about our deeper expression of love—what you would
call sex. Let us now briefly discuss how we Lemurians
join in divine union. Please know you on the surface
have been taught a great deal of shame and distortion
associated with the topic of sex. This is a result of your
lost connection to the divine, which is in the process
of shifting.

Please know how we experience the union of physical
sex would not actually be considered your sexual
intercourse in the three-dimensional world. Remember
we were/are a combination of physical and light bodies
and a balance of the masculine and feminine energies,
leaning more toward what you would consider feminine.
Thus, most of our divine union is/was experienced
in our light body through the unity frequency of
unconditional love. There is neither controlling,
needs, nor manipulation in the sexual act. We shift
our frequency (at will) from higher to lower in order
to become denser so we can experience the physical
combining of our bodies. This also allows the union of
sperm and egg in our denser bodies, as the orgasm was/
is experienced in all our bodies spiritually, emotionally,
mentally, and physically. You experience some of this

in your peak moment of orgasm, but it fades quickly. We maintain and sustain that feeling for an extended period.

To outsiders, including the Atlanteans, our sexual practices would appear open, free, and a joyful expression of all aspects of our selves. We allow the sexual experience to be a way to experience the bliss of life while connecting with higher realms (sometimes you in 3-D just get high). There is never any shame associated with our intimacy.

When the important decision is made to manifest a child, this is achieved through a thought-out process of connecting with the spirit that wishes to incarnate and connecting with their divine soul plan. We make sure there is a match with the parents to support that plan. Since our life spans were/are long, this is/was an important decision for parent and child. The sperm meeting the egg just may be the only similarity that takes place in how our two worlds have sex. We have neither unwanted pregnancies nor children having children. Bringing a child into physical format is considered one of the most sacred acts. Soon, you too will return to this form of true, divine sexual union.

- Phillip, with The Lemurian Council of 12.

Lemurian Council Message #14:

WHY DID OUR GOLDEN AGE END?

Many have asked how and why the Lemurian Golden Age ended. Having been such an advanced civilization, how could this possibly happen and why? This is an important question and answer for your world to ponder and from which to learn. Many Golden Ages before and after us failed. It is your destiny to create one that does not in order to fully move into your master teacher ship within the universe. From our ending, your America is destined to be a final Golden Age so your planet and humanity can and will ascend to their divine destiny. Listen and learn as we attempt to explain to your mental and emotional bodies what happened and why. Dear Ones, in your hearts you already know what we are about to explain. You were there!

When Lemuria was ending as we had known it (some were allowed to preserve our wisdoms and move into the Inner Earth realms so you would have a way back home), our connections with each other and the universe also ended. While our foundation collapsed, our eternal bond with you on the surface was never lost, as our connection was stored in eternal light (encoded in the Inner Earth central sun's DNA), and you are in the process of rebooting that connection

with us and other higher realms at this time (your ascension).

During our great civilization, we never allowed ourselves to be immersed totally in physical form for fear of losing our spiritual connection. Most of the time, we experienced existence in our light bodies but did have the ability to move into our denser physical bodies at times, especially during reproduction. You on the surface are fully in physical form and have learned all there is to know from that experience... the good, the bad, the ugly, as they say. Now you need to accomplish what we could not: a balance of the spiritual and the physical.

Now your mission, if you so choose, is to recapture your divinity, the most sacred, essential part of you and integrate it into the physical. In later messages we shall continue to support you in attaining your next evolutionary ascension steps...

Let's now go over some details to better assist you in understanding/remembering what happened in our past.

In addition to the centuries of attacks, enslavements, and scientific experimentation, and inner marriages by the assertive masculine energy of the Atlanteans (we Lemurians were/are receptive feminine energy not interested in confrontation), the planet, Mother Earth,

was still having growing pains. More than you have ever experienced, the tectonic plates were shifting with much volcanic activity, earthquakes, and tidal waves. We were foretold many eons in advance that our continent would be completely destroyed as part of the planet's reconfiguration.

So when the final time came, some of us chose to return to our home galaxy, while others received permission from the Universal Council Federation to ascend into a higher frequency within the planet, while others migrated to Atlantis and other parts of the world. At this time, many aspects of our Lemurian culture were spread throughout the planet but never in the full force of our original civilization. This is a book unto itself.

Some of these cultures are names you still know today: Egypt, Inca, Mayan, Hopi, Easter Island, Native American, and many that have been lost in your reality of time. Over one hundred also exist in higher realms within the Inner Earth Agartha civilizations. The reality of this will be soon revealed to those not now aware of that which we speak.

The frequency of the planet was becoming denser and less filled with light, as humanity chose to separate from God and do things their own way. This began your separation from self and others and your long

path of duality and confrontation. The end time of this has now come at long last.

We wish to repeat (repetition is a good learning tool for your mental bodies), before the destruction of our life, much of our wisdom was saved for us and you so you would have a way back home (connection to ALL THERE IS). Knowledge was stored from the Inner Earth central sun in crystalline light libraries and temples, and you are now discovering these truths through the activation of certain vortices/portals on the surface.

We have waited in a higher frequency for many millennia for us to now unite and create the final Golden Age that does not have to die...so you/we can go out into the universe and be the master teachers we are destined to be. That is what this has all been about, Dear Ones! You have learned all there is to know from 'what is not.' Now, hand and hand, let us take 'what is' (your god-self within) and spread that light through the many worlds that need it.

- Phillip, with The Lemurian Council of 12

Lemurian Council Message #15:

YOU STILL NEED TO GET BACK HOME

Dear Hearts, in Message #14 we spoke about the reasons Lemuria failed because we were fearful/unable to completely inhabit physical/human bodies for fear of losing our connection to ALL THERE IS, along with the negative Atlantean and shifting Earth influences.

We revisit all this now so you may choose to learn from it and not have to learn the same way we did. We failed to know that to be completely human was our true mission (a balance of spiritual and physical) while being able to access the divine. Does this sound familiar now?

So, in many ways, our mission was never fully completed being totally human while at the same time embracing our spiritual beingness. It is now up to you to complete what we could not, if you so choose through your freedom of will and choice, Dear Ones. Because our genetic coding is the same, and many of you lived in Lemuria; the Lemuria Life is still alive within humanity. Can you feel it?

Through the ages since our demise, many aspects of Lemuria have remained within humanity on the surface of the planet. Let us review some of these as a way to expand your ascension process and see if you

can see the connection between us...as your way back
home...

Things we still have in common:

The need to create communities of equality, harmony,
and balance; the need to know who you are and why
you are here; to know your talents and gifts and how
to bring them into world service; moving from the me
to the we consciousness; to heal the me (emotionally,
mentally, and physically) and not transfer the
unhealed me into the we; to honor all aspects of
Mother Earth; to know and apply Universal Law; to
connect with higher realms; to establish and maintain
world peace; to awaken the god-self; to end duality
and separation and lack and limitation; to apply
ancient wisdom's now; to understand the connection
of all life; to honor your physical body; to create
sacred journeys to specific vortices, etc., etc...

Many of these sound very familiar to you, don't
they? We are indeed one, Dear Ones. Your United
States of America was founded on many of the above
principles by your founding fathers who were in direct
connection with us. Your America will be your entry
into the next Golden Age no matter how things appear
on the outside now. It is your destiny.

We all have unique, individual divine soul plans that
will allow all to create a reality that will and can

include many of the above wisdoms... it's just a matter of when.

Let us now join hands, as light workers and way showers, and together finally complete our mission to be human and connected to ALL THERE IS. What do you choose, Dear Ones?

- Phillip, with The Lemurian Council of 12.

Lemurian Council Message #16:

OUR TRUE TEMPLE, THE BODY

As we have discussed, the Lemurian body was/is composed of two distinct parts: the light and the physical bodies. Yours is also, but you are mainly stuck in experiencing the physical. This is all shifting as you embrace your multidimensionality.

Since our light bodies allowed us to reach far out into universal wisdom and reality, we learned to listen to our bodies as a great teaching tool. Our bodies were/are our greatest teaching tool. We are sad to see how little most of you on the surface think and feel about your bodies. Remember your bodies house your spirit/soul, but most of you don't think of that aspect much either. This is now changing as your vibrations increase during the gift of the ascension process (moving to a higher realm of reality).

There were/are many means we Lemurians employ to keep our light and physical bodies at the highest frequency possible. Many of these you know, and we invite you to use them daily: the use of breath, sound, and motion through meditation, exercise, and controlled breathing; eating high vibrational, live food (where no life force is totally destroyed); drinking pure water; consuming no alcohol; emotional,

mental, and physical clearing and cleansing (a personal process); connecting to nature/Mother Earth; joyful, divine sexual union; resting whenever necessary; and a balance of work and play.

Being aware of your emotions and thoughts and how they create balance and imbalances in your body is essential. Your medical community is beginning to connect your emotions and thoughts with your diseases, aging, and what you call death.

We were/are able to maintain and sustain long periods of life in one body and/or immortality by conquering our emotions and thoughts. You are in the process of recapturing this ability. Once you master this, you will be free of disease, aging, and death.

This is going to be so wonderful for you!!

- Phillip, with the Lemurian Council of 12.

Lemurian Council Message #17:

UNIVERSAL LAW: THE BACKBONE OF THE
UNIVERISE AND LEMURIA

One of the most 'downgrading' aspects that the 3-D
world has experienced is your lost contact with the
fundamentals of something called 'Universal Law.'
This downgrade was the result of the abuse of this law
in the past. As you rediscover these principles, let us
affirm you will not repeat your past.

The truth of this law is that everything is
interconnected. What affects one affects all. This law
is the element that holds the entire universe together.
What appears to you as dark, empty outer space is
actually filled with the consciousness of this truth and
law. This consciousness, this force of energy, includes
everything physical and unseen nonphysical. In
effect, it is the manifestation of Creative Source, and
everything you can and cannot see is maintained and
sustained through Universal Law.

All aspects of the universe are a 'Unified Field' and
associate with each other even if they are in different
dimensions. Thus, ALL THERE IS is connected to
itself in a limitless energy field we call the universe
(one version, oneness, unity). The universe is ever-
growing and expanding through the creativity of
the Creator with no end through Universal Law. For

the sake of these short messages, we are speaking in simplistic terms, and the actual 'science' of that which we speak can fill libraries.

In Lemuria we had/have chosen to stay connected with Universal Law and knew the energy of our thoughts, emotions, intentions, and actions vibrated throughout the universe and affected the Law. Our telepathic ability allowed us to be constantly conscious of the interconnection of everything. Since we knew what others were thinking, untruth was not a part of our reality. Can you imagine if deceit and the denial of deceit were eliminated from your world? What a different world you would have. Well, you can have that reality again, if you so choose.

Through Universal Law we knew there was no ownership of anything or anyone (no control). We are/ were stewards for a specific period of allotted time. Another component of the Law is freedom of choice and will, where no other force other than you can affect your soul plan within a civilization of equality, harmony, and balance.

Once you reconnect with this Universal Law, the joy and the bliss of your life will return, and you will leave lack and limitation and duality behind forevermore!

- Phillip, with The Lemurian Council of 12.

Lemurian Council Message #18:

UNIVERSAL CHOICE VS. UNIVERSAL LAW

In message #17 we spoke of the connection to ALL THERE IS through Universal Law. But when we and other advanced civilizations on this planet choose to lose our connection to Universal Law (moving from the heart that knows to the mind that believes), we might call that Universal Choice. Since all beings on Earth have a freedom of choice and will (that no one can tamper with), the Universal Law of Unity/We Consciousness was never forced at any time. We were, in effect, choosing to learn what is through what is not—a tough way to learn but a way. You on the surface of this world have embraced and continued this teaching tool for eons. But that timeline/end time has come. Through duality, separation, and confrontation, you have gone as far from yourself, one another, and Source as you can go. Have not you, Dear Ones? There are many teachings, once again, coming to you to balance this situation. In the past you have killed and destroyed teachers bringing you the truth. Allowing the alter ego within the mental body to be assertive has created much of your negative past. Are you willing to accept with compassion and forgive how you have chosen to learn in the past and present and move into a new way of being and learning?

Now through the ascension process, the mind is
moving into service to the heart—the heart that
knows, the mind that believes (and beliefs shift and
change, but truth/knowing remains constant). We are
not speaking of eliminating the mind but have it work
in balance with the heart. They both have many things
to contribute. The reason this heart/mind balance
is happening is due to the reality that the planet has
chosen to ascend; thus, everything within and upon
her body needs to do the same. And this includes you,
Dear Ones. Only through the loving heart can this
take place—a heart that cannot shame, blame, nor
judge neither self nor others and sees all in equality,
harmony, and balance. You are learning to think
with your hearts, Dear Ones, and create a new world
paradigm.

Here are some qualities of the 'knowing heart' that
are supporting your personal and planetary ascension
processes. Many of these teachings you have been
taught in the past/present and ignored them. Are you
ready to see the meaning, value, and purpose in them
and embrace them at long last?

Qualities of the knowing heart: equality, harmony, and
balance; acceptance, compassion, and forgiveness;
unconditional love; balance of giving and receiving;
gratitude for what is allowing abundance; trust
and surrender to higher realms and the unknown
(allowing the probability and possibility of

manifestation); releasing attachment to drama and glamour as a comfort zone; not choosing negativity and confrontation; living in the now moment; being conscious/aware; being in joy and blessing for life and all living things; being open to learn from sources other than the human mind.

And these are just a few, most likely not new, for there are many aspects of the heart. There are many books and teachings on these wondrous qualities, but you get the idea. These qualities are essential in building your new world paradigm. The existing old-world paradigm is dying right before your very eyes. Have you noticed?

Through your freedom of will and choice and resonance and discernment we shall leave it up to you. Are you ready to raise your individual vibration and thus that of your world so our two worlds can join in one? This portion of our higher frequency world was saved in order to show you the way back home. Then we can show you wonders beyond your imagination that will thrill and delight you and connect you once again to the universe. Are you ready, Dear Ones, to commit to creating a new you and world—a world that never has to be destroyed again?

- Phillip, with The Lemurian Council of 12

Lemurian Council Message #19:

SACRED VORTICES AND JOURNEYS

For eons the peoples of this planet have sought and journeyed to and worked within sacred vortices/ portals/sites. Many ancient temples and towns were located along these energetic grids connected to Inner Earth and the universe energies. The bodies of you, the Earth, and the universe are connected to these vortices, allowing empowerment and regeneration and healing. Soon the complete science of all this will be revealed again.

Allow this message to serve as a brief discussion.

Most of the vortices on this planet were originally discovered by Lemurians and later used through subsequent civilizations, such as Atlantean, Egyptian, Mayan, Incan, Hopi, Greek, Roman, etc. These post-Lemurian cultures, in a more limited way, maintained and sustained much of the limited knowledge you have today about these sacred sites. The pyramids of Egypt, Mexico, Peru, and Stonehenge are built on such energy centers. Most have been lost in time, but many are reactivating at this time and becoming physical in view. Recent vortex discoveries include ones on the North and South Poles (entry portals to the Inner Earth) and in the Caribbean Sea. This is happening due to the ascension process of the planet and the wisdoms

within these sites that are meant to come forward at this special time to support humanity within their process.

Advanced ancient science employed sacred geometry and connection to cosmic consciousness, which allowed us to locate, create, and activate these sacred vortices/sites/portals. There is actually a worldwide network (your cyber worldwide web is a weak reflection of this) of these sacred sites all connected to one another, the Inner Earth, and cosmic energies. In your future you will develop a limitless, free source of energy for your world from these sites. This change to the financial structure of your world will assist in creating unity consciousness and show you do not own or control anything in your world.

Let us review some of the gifts gained from these sacred vortices/sites/portals: connecting various networks to each other and the cosmos; assisting the planet and humanity within the ascension process; activating past and present cellular memories; assisting personal growth allowing global growth; shifting the emotional, mental, and physical bodies from carbon to crystalline existence; activating multidimensional abilities; and revealing blueprints for our way back into advanced civilization...just to name a few.

Remember each sacred vortex is situated on its own grid of energy or energy center. Each vortex is unique

and contributes its uniqueness to the whole network of vortices. At this time several of these vortices are being activated a day due to the energies coming into the Earth plane and from within (as above, so below). Humanity is downloading much wisdom as a result of this. You are reconnecting with your Source and Universal Laws to empower you into your next Golden Age.

Visiting these vortices can be a life transforming, transitioning, and healing event for you, the planet, and all peoples of this world. Many of you are serving as proxies for humanity and being and doing vital work at these vortices.

These vortices/sacred sites are a wonder-filled way for us to connect now until you are ready to complete your ascension process so that we may finally connect physically and at long last become one.

- Phillip, with The Lemurian Council of 12

Lemurian Council Message #20:

IN CONCLUSION

Whether you believe Lemuria was a real place or not does not matter. You can see it as myth or fact. What matters is the intention and teaching within the messages. The question is: if you don't believe the messenger exists, does that discredit the value, meaning, and purpose of the message? We shall leave it up to your resonance and discernment and freedom of will and choice. The answer lies within your hearts, Dear Ones, not in your minds. But may we remind you that great teachings exist in both fiction and nonfiction. And good fiction is most often based upon nonfiction.

The reason we have transmitted these messages is to briefly review who we are and why we are here and to reveal our successes and failures in order to give you a loving pathway back home. Our genetic coding and destinies are combined; what affects you, affects us; we are truly one (and so is the entire universe). Your path now will not be the same as your past. It cannot be and you survive. It will be through the creation of a new you and world. The old you and world is dying, Dear Ones. This new paradigm will be you fully loving you, thus others, and truly knowing where you came from and where you are headed. You are creating communities of equality, harmony, and balance as you move from a

'me' consciousness to a 'we' consciousness of unity and oneness.

Allow these words we have given again at this time to be an inspiration to accept with compassion, thus forgive, your past path and way now back home. For, Dear Ones, you really never fully left home. You have been dropping bread crumbs all along the way to find your way back into your divine essence. See each of the messages as one of the crumbs you dropped to follow...

Your planet has already shifted into a higher consciousness; thus, all upon and within her body must do the same. You are now all being given a unique opportunity—all nine billion of you. Why do you think you are here now? It isn't because you have advanced so far but that you are ready to truly advance. You are all being given a choice through your free will and choice. No one has to do this. What do you choose?

The space between our dimensions is very thin now; we are closer than ever before. Many of you can feel and even see us. But that doesn't matter. Again, what matters are the messages we bring to assist you to complete the leap to your higher destiny. You are destined to lead the way into your planet's next Golden Age, which can be the final one that does not have to be destroyed like others and ours.

The path begins and ends within each of you. This is a process from inside out, not outside in. You now hold a vital choice to make. Are you ready? Where are you in this process? Are you committed to fully activating your individual soul and planetary plans? The choice has always been yours...

- Phillip, with The Lemurian Council of 12

Resources

Phillip Elton Collins
The Angel News Network
www.TheAngelNewsNetwork.com

The Modern Day Mystery School, Fort Lauderdale, Florida
www.TheModernDayMysterySchool.com

Also by Phillip Elton Collins:
Coming Home to Lemuria: An Ascension Adventure Story
Order via: www.TheAngelNewsNetwork.com.

Books

The Ascension Handbook by Joel D. Anastasi with Channel Jessie Keener
Order via: www.TheAngelNewsNetwork.com.

Life Mastery by Joel D. Anastasi with Channel Jeff Fasano
Order via: www.TheAngelNewsNetwork.com.

The Second Coming by Joel D. Anastasi with Channel Robert Baker (iUniverse)
Order via: www.GabrielSecondComing.com.

The Emerald Tablets by Ashalyn and Thoth the Atlantean
Order via: www.emeraldtablets.net.

Journey of the Awakened Heart by Jeff Fasano with
Stephanie Gunning
Order via: www.TheAngelNewsNetwork.com.

Telos & Messages from the Hollow Earth by Dianne
Robbins, Inner Earth Books
Order via: www.DianneRobbins.com.

Websites

Pulitzer Prize For Poetry
www.pulitzerprizeforpoetry.org

The Poetry Foundation
www.poets.org

Academy of American Poets
www.poets.org

Children of Light (Archangel Gabriel/Robert Baker)
www.ChildrenofLight.com.

Mary Liz Murphy
www.lifeforcesolutions.com.

Shambhala Center
www.crystal-skulls-mayan.com.

About the Author

My entire life has been in preparation for this book. I am now able to receive these extraordinary truths and teachings and give them to you. This is a true balance of giving and receiving—an important aspect of all of our divine soul plans.

As cofounder of The Angel News Network and The Modern Day Mystery School, I am a healing arts therapist, workshop facilitator, and life coach.

My professional background is a multidimensional mixture that includes being a journalist; having an extensive advertising career at Young & Rubicam, New York City; being founder of Fairbanks Films with film directors Ridley and Tony Scott; being director of marketing at Industrial Light & Magic Commercials/Lucasfilm, representing some the world's most talented film directors; as well as thousands of hours of clinical experience and teaching of advanced metaphysics and healing arts.

As an ordained minister within the Order of Melchizedek, I am also a conscious channel for many higher realms throughout the universe. My book *COMING HOME TO LEMURIA: AN ASCENSION ADVENTURE STORY* is another example of higher realms connections.

It is my passion to integrate the seen and unseen worlds through the talents and gifts I have been given. This is a crucial time for our species and planet, and I am humbled to be of service. It is my intention that you resonate with the wisdoms presented in these poems and messages and are able to personally apply them and perhaps take them out into the world yourself.